T/R1105

RAILWAY BYLINES

ANNUAL No.6

A splendid line-up of works shunters at Wolverton on 7 April 1957. We suspect that the one in the middle is the famous EARLESTOWN. PHOTOGRAPH: THE TRANSPORT TREASURY

RAILWAY BYLINES

Editor
Martin Smith

All correspondence regarding editorial matters
should be addressed to;
RAILWAY BYLINES
P.O.BOX 1957, RADSTOCK, BATH BA3 5YJ
Tel: 01373-812048
(office hours only please)
Fax: 01373-813610
E-mail: smudger@ivycot49.freeserve.co.uk
Views expressed by contributors are not necessarily those of
the editor or publisher. Information is published in good faith,
but no liability can be accepted for loss or inconvenience
arising from error or omission.
The editor will be pleased to consider contributions
(articles, photographs or whatever) for publication but, while
every reasonable care will be taken, no responsibility can be
accepted for loss or damage, howsoever caused.
In the case of manuscripts submitted for publication, the
editor reserves the right to amend the text, if necessary, to suit
the style of the magazine. Where possible, edited/amended
texts will be returned to the contributor for his/her approval,
but the final decision rests with the editor.

The magazine RAILWAY BYLINES is
published monthly by Irwell Press Ltd.,
59a High Street, Clophill, Beds MK45 4BE. It
is printed in Luton by JetSpeed and
distributed by COMAG, London.
All distribution enquiries regarding the
NEWSTRADE and MODEL SHOPS should be
directed to Magazine Subscriptions, PO
Box 464, Berkhamsted, Herts HP4 2UR.
COPYRIGHT IRWELL PRESS 2003
ALL RIGHTS RESERVED
This book printed by
The Amadeus Press, Bradford U.K. 2003

Main cover picture: N10 69109 turns on the 'table at Bowes Bridge
shed on the Tanfield branch, some time in 1960. PHOTOGRAPH:
ALAN R.THOMPSON

Upper cover picture: Kerr Stuart 0-4-0WT CROOKES at ICI
Silvertown, 14 March 1959. PHOTOGRAPH: JOHN R.BONSER

Top right. One of the charismatic ex-GNSR D40s near
Tillynaught with a train from Banff *circa* 1950/51.
PHOTOGRAPH: THE TRANSPORT TREASURY

Below right. 67200 at Ongar on 6 October 1957. This was the last
full month of steam working between Epping and Ongar as the
Central Line electrics took over on 18 November.
PHOTOGRAPH: A.E.BENNETT

Above. The old Fletcher Jennings-built water tower at Moor Row
shed – or to be precise what remained of Moor Row shed (not
much, actually) – on 15 March 1969. Despite this scene of
abandonment, the trackbed through the nearby Moor Row station
was later converted to a cycleway-cum-footpath. The old station
platforms are still there, one either side of the cycleway. (At
least, they were still there when your editor visited in September
2002.) PHOTOGRAPH: F.W.SHUTTLEWORTH

Rear cover photo: LMS Express Parcels – was the horse fed 'go-
faster' oats? The location is the rear of Craddocks shoe warehouse
at Snow Hill, Wolverhampton, and the date is 18 September 1952.
PHOTOGRAPH: F.W.SHUTTLEWORTH

CONTENTS

THE TANFIELD BRANCH – THE OLDEST EXISTING RAILWAY IN THE WORLD
by Alan R.Thompson

N10 69100 shunts at the top of Lobley Hill Incline. The engine appears to have steam brakes only so this would date the picture to pre-May 1954. The train is passing over the Whickham-Lobley Hill road (B6317) level crossing; the crossing wheel can be seen in the signal box. PHOTOGRAPH: J.W.ARMSTRONG TRUST

'The question of the world's oldest railway has always been a debatable one, and although there is some evidence as to the existence of wagonways prior to the opening of the Tanfield Railway, there is no doubt that the honours must go to this branch as the oldest surviving *railway in the world'.* T.E.Rounthwaite writing in the *Railway Observer,* 1958.

Coal had been mined on the banks of the River Tyne for many years, but by the early 1600s many of these easily-worked seams which were close to the surface were becoming exhausted so the mining proprietors started looking inland for further coal measures to work. However, one major problem in developing coal reserves inland was that of transportation. Roads were very poor – they were little more than dirt tracks, dusty in summer and bogged down with mud in the winter – and were far from ideal for moving large quantities of coal by horse and basket, the favoured mode of transport at that time. Given the state of the roads, the progression to horse and cart was little better. But the next progression *did* offer much more promise – this was the 'waggonway' whereby the carts were equipped with flanged wheels

so that they could run on wooden rails. One of the first waggonways was in the Gateshead area; known as the Whickham Way, it was in use from around 1620 to about 1705. Eventually, a vast network of wooden-railed waggonways was constructed throughout the area so that coal from inland pits could be taken to the Tyne for loading into ships.

This construction and use of waggonways might sound fairly straightforward, but there was a fly in the ointment. The waggonways operated, not with an Act of Parliament, but under 'wayleaves' whereby a rental was paid to the owners of the land over which the lines were constructed – usually so much per loaded wagon. The landowners were well aware that there were vast profits to be made from the sale of coal and this often led to extortionate rental demands. Some

coal owners countered this by banding together to build their own waggonway running over land which they had purchased. The subject of this article, the Tanfield Waggonway, was the result of such a collaboration between what were known as the 'Grand Allies': the Liddells of Ravensworth, the Cotesworths of Whickham, the Wortleys of Gibside and Causey and eventually George Bowes of Marley and Hedley. This became one of the greatest partnerships in the entire coal industry, and the names of Liddell, Wortley, Cotesworth and Bowes are well-remembered to this day.

The Tanfield Waggonway
The Tanfield Waggonway was built to gain access to the rich coal seams existing in the Tanfield Moor area near Stanley where good quality coal was comparatively easily worked. Hitherto, coal from this area had been transported via a line which was usually known as the Main Way – it started in the Pontop area and ran downhill north towards Burnopfield then followed the River Derwent to the Tyne at Derwenthaugh.

Construction of the Tanfield Waggonway started in 1723. The northern section was built largely on the trackbed of the old Whickham Way from Dunston

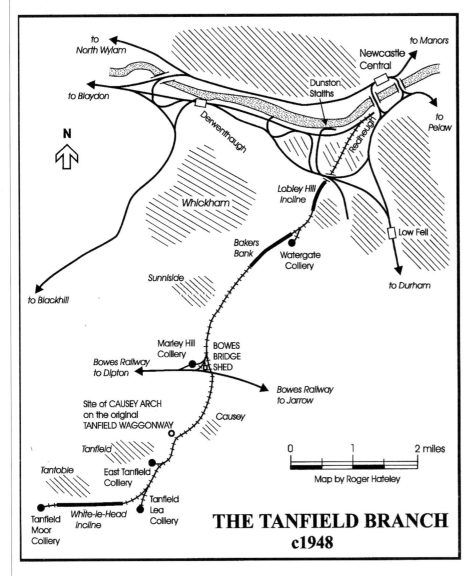

**THE TANFIELD BRANCH
c1948**

Map by Roger Hateley

Still in the first half of the 1950s but up at the other end of the line, N10 69090 heads past East Tanfield with a load of empties for Tanfield Lea Colliery. The train is crossing the road between Tanfield village and Stanley. The ruins on the right are the old colliery brick works.PHOTOGRAPH:J.W.ARMSTRONG TRUST

up to Lobley Hill, but a new section to Sunniside was added by 1724 and this was extended to Causey by 1725. Another new section was laid from Lobley Hill northwards via Redheugh to new staiths on the river; these staiths were part of the Liddell family empire.

To reach a colliery known as Dawsons Pit near Tanfield and also to access one or two other small pits, a branch was laid from a point near Causey. This branch achieved lasting fame in that it required the building of the Causey Arch, which is generally acknowledged as Britain's first railway bridge. Completed in 1727 to the design of Ralph Wood, a local mason, the bridge had a 105ft span and was some 80ft above the burn. Not only was it pioneering in railway terms, but it also had the largest single span in Britain at the time and, indeed, retained that status for another 30 years. Unfortunately for our railway history, the Causey branch did not last too long – it closed in 1740 (some sources state 1780), having become redundant due to a fire at the colliery it served. However, the famous Causey Arch still survives today as a listed structure in the care of Durham County Council.

Another branch ran from Causey to serve pits at Shield Row, Kip Hill and Beamish South Moor. This followed the

25-inch Ordnance Survey map, 1938. The Tanfield branch passes between Bowes Bridge engine shed and the turntable and exits at the bottom right-hand corner of the map. Marley Hill Colliery, although connected to the Tanfield Branch, dispatched its coal via the Bowes Railway, the connection to which was to the west of the colliery. CROWN COPYRIGHT

approximate line of what is now the present day road from Sunniside to Stanley, the A6076. There was one further extension to the waggonway. This was made in the 1820s* and was also from Causey. It ran down the east bank of the Causey Burn to East Tanfield and Tanfield Lea to serve new pits which were being developed in this area. (*It has been suggested elsewhere that this section did not appear until the line was developed by the Brandling Junction Railway – q.v.).

Engineering feats

The land in the Tanfield and Causey area is some 700-800 ft above the River Tyne but is only some 8 or 9 miles distant. Consequently, the waggonway had a considerable overall climb and also had to cross various valleys and ridges along the way. The waggonway had a multitude of engineering features well in excess of anything that had been attempted before, and indeed formed the basis of railway civil engineering as we know it today. The building of Causey Arch wasn't the only major civil engineering feat – spoil from deep cuttings was used to build the world's first railway embankment which was some 100ft high and over 300ft wide at the base over Causey Burn. All this was to keep gradients to a minimum – apart from two inclines (one at Bakers Bank and the other at Lobley Hill), the ruling gradient was a comparatively modest 1 in 40.

The waggonway was built to the gauge of 4ft. It appears that, in anticipation of heavy traffic, it was double track from the very outset – a 'main way' for loaded wagons and a 'bye way' for returning empties. The anticipation became realisation . The volume of traffic was such that, during the 18th Century, the Tanfield Waggonway was acknowledged as being by far the largest coal carrier in Britain – it is on record that, in 1732, some 400 loaded horse-drawn chaldron wagons (carrying a total of over 1,000 tons of coal) passed along the line each day to the quay at Dunston for shipment. As new pits opened, that figure steadily increased.

New proprietors

In 1836 an agreement was reached with the Brandling Junction Railway to rebuild the Tanfield Waggonway as an 'iron' railway. After one false start, the upgrading work was finally put in hand in February 1839. It was fully completed in November 1841, having cost a total of £14,000. The upgrading of the line brought some new traffic to the waggonway. Tanfield Moor Colliery had originally dispatched its coal via the 'Main Way' to Derwenthaugh but had been diverted to the Stanhope & Tyne Railway at Annfield Plain in 1834; however, with the upgrading of the Tanfield Waggonway an agreement was reached for the Tanfield Moor coal to be conveyed over the Tanfield Waggonway. To provide the necessary connection between the colliery and the existing waggonway a self-acting incline was constructed at Tanfield Moor down the hill to Tanfield Lea.

The upgrading of the waggonway also prompted the introduction, in June 1842,

Tanfield Moor Colliery closed in 1948. This picture which looks west was taken in 1950 but, clearly, the place had already become very derelict. PHOTOGRAPH: T.ROUNTHWAITE; E.B.MAXWELL COLLECTION

of a passenger service on the line. This service, which operated only on Saturdays, ran from Tanfield Lea to Gateshead, stopping only at Bowes Bridge and Bakers Bank; the outward trip left Tanfield Lea at 9am with the return journey starting at 4pm. Initially a coach was used for this service but it was later replaced by an ordinary goods wagon fitted with plank seats! The precise date of the cessation of this service is unknown, but it seems to have had only a short life.

There was another administrative change in 1845 when the Brandling Junction Railway became part of the Newcastle & Darlington Junction Railway. That company eventually became the York Newcastle & Berwick Railway which, in 1854, became part of the newly-formed North Eastern Railway. Thus the Tanfield line became one of only a few wooden-railed waggonways which ended up as part of a 'main line' public railway system.

Locomotives

Despite the upgrading of the line and the various corporate changes, the Tanfield line remained in the 'pre-locomotive' era for some time. The level sections of the line were horse-worked, the inclines at Bowes Bridge and Causey Woods were worked by steam winding engines while the inclines at Lobley Hill, Bakers Bank and Tanfield Moor (otherwise known as White-le-Heads) were self-acting.

However, that changed on 1 July 1881 when steam locomotives were introduced on the line. Or, to be precise, on *parts* of the line. Locomotives started to take over from horses, not only on the level sections, but also on the inclines which had been worked by stationary winding engines. However, the self acting inclines at Lobley Hill, Bakers Bank and Tanfield Moor were retained. The old winding engine house at Bowes Bridge was converted for use as an engine shed.

There are few surviving records of the types of locomotives used in the early days, but it seems pretty certain that various NER 0-6-0Ts were originally used. From 1891 the 'L' class (LNER J73) 0-6-0Ts started to appear on the line and, in the early 1900s, N and U class (LNER N9 and N10) 0-6-2Ts made their debut. The N10s became the regular engines (albeit occasionally augmented by J25 0-6-0s) and retained that status for most of the line's life. That said, it is known that on at least one occasion a J21 0-6-0 was based at Bowes Bridge; this was presumably at a time when other engines were unavailable, the parent shed at Gateshead simply sending whatever authorised engine it could muster.

In LNER days the level section between the foot of Lobley Hill Incline and Redheugh was the domain of J71 and J72 0-6-0Ts. The bank from Redheugh up to

continued on page 10

The level crossing near the Causey Arch had a crossing keeper in residence, but it was hardly a demanding job in the line's later years. N10 69090 approaches with a train heading downhill to Tanfield Lea. PHOTOGRAPH: J.W.ARMSTRONG TRUST

The famous Causey Arch over Causey Burn – the world's first railway bridge. Sadly it had only a short railway life, but it still stands today. This picture was taken on 24 March 1991. PHOTOGRAPH: IAN S.CARR

At Marley Hill, the Tanfield line was crossed on the level by the Bowes Railway. This general view of the crossing shows the small signal box which had been provided by the NER. In the background are two rows of colliery housing – Gibraltar Row and Marley Hill Terrace – which were for the miners employed at Marley Hill Colliery. 69090 heads a load of coal empties for Tanfield Lea. One of the wagons seems to be carrying timber – this was sometimes brought in by rail for maintenance purposes. PHOTOGRAPH: J.W.ARMSTRONG TRUST

The original engine shed at Bowes Bridge had been converted from a winding house. Its origins are not difficult to see, especially with the chimney. This picture was taken on 5 May 1935. N9 1643 (designated BR 69415 but withdrawn before having its new number applied) and N10 1138 (later BR 69100) are on shed. The shed burned down in 1943. PHOTOGRAPH: A.R.THOMPSON COLLECTION

69109 drifts past the remains of Bowes Bridge shed with a load of empties in the early 1950s. As noted in the text a new shed was not erected until 1954/55. In the interim, the only option was to stable the engines in the open. PHOTOGRAPH: J.W.ARMSTRONG TRUST

For the Information and Guidance of Railway Officers and Railway Staff only.

BRITISH RAILWAYS
(North Eastern Operating Area)

DIVISIONAL OPERATING SUPERINTENDENT,
YORK.

O.4040   4th September, 1953.

TANFIELD BRANCH

INSTRUCTIONS REGARDING THE WORKING OF ENGINES AND WAGONS
UP OR DOWN LOBLEY HILL INCLINE

_____

When it is necessary for an engine or train to be worked up Lobley Hill Incline by Locomotive Power, the following arrangements must be made before the train or engine is allowed to leave the Teams Yard.

1. The rope must be correctly laid by the Bank Rider at the Bank Head for the line upon which the train or engine is intended to run.

2. All points which become facing must be placed in the proper position by the Bank Rider at the Bank Head for the movement about to be made.

3. The facing points at the Bank Foot leading to Dunston Forge must be secured by clamp by the leading man at Bank Foot in the proper position towards the incline.

4. The Bank Rider at the Bank Head must proceed down the incline and satisfy himself that all facing points for the movement are correctly set, that the line is clear of any obstruction, and that the rope has been correctly laid to allow the passage of the train or engine up the incline.
The Bank Rider at the Bank Foot or another member of the incline staff instructed by the Leading man at Teams Yard, if the Bank Rider is not available, must assist in the placing of the rope and securing of points.

5. The Bank Rider from the Bank Head will, after satisfying himself that the incline is in order for the train or engine to proceed, advise the Leading man at the Teams Yard, who will inform the Teams Crossing Keeper and the Guard, or Driver in the case of a light engine. The train or engine must not depart until the proper fixed signal for the movement has been placed in the clear position by the Crossing Keeper at Teams Crossing, who must obtain the permission of the Leading man at Teams Yard before placing the appropriate fixed signal in the clear position. The Bank Rider must ride on the engine to the Bank Top.

6. The maximum gross load to be worked up the incline by one Class N.10 engine is 40 tons.

7. In the event of it being necessary for an engine or train to proceed down the incline in emergency without the rope, similar arrangements must be made, but the Bank Foot Bank Rider will walk the incline to the Bank Head and ride on the engine on the downward journey.

8. An engine must be at the lower end when a vehicle or vehicles are worked over the incline by locomotive power.

A. P. HUNTER,
(O.3024).   Divisional Operating Superintendent.

Gateshead usually warranted the attendance of two engines; until the early part of the 20th Century purpose-built Fletcher 0-6-0STs had been used there but, in LNER days, J73s were the usual engines.

The inclines

As mentioned earlier, despite the introduction of locomotive working in 1881 the Tanfield branch retained three self acting inclines:

• White-le-Head (also known as Tanfield Moor) – 1,850 yards in length; starting gradient of 1 in 9 but most of it was between 1 in 15 and 1 in 20; three men employed

• Bakers Bank (sometimes referred to as Sunniside or Fugar Bar) – one mile in length; steepest section 1 in 11; an LNER report dated 1927 states that the staff comprised 1 Leadingman (basic rate of pay 65/-), 3 Bankriders (64/-) and 1 Bankman (junior pay scale)

• Lobley Hill – approximately 1,400 yards in length; principally at 1 in 16 with a curve to the north and another back to the east; in 1927 the staff comprised 1 Leadingman and 3 Bankriders, their basic rates of pay being the same as their counterparts at Baker's Bank.

The operation of each of the three inclines was similar. A $1^1/4$ in-diameter steel rope ran the full length of the incline; it rested on a series of guiding rollers and sheaves, some set horizontally with others at an angle or vertical. The rope passed around two wheels – a binding wheel and a brake wheel – set into the ground at the head of the incline. The brake wheel was 16ft in diameter and was fitted with a drum; the working of the incline was controlled by a bankman or brakesman from a cabin at the top of the incline. Loaded wagons were attached to the rope at the head of the incline and, when descending, their weight was used to draw

The new Bowes Bridge shed of 1954/55, photographed in 1960. N10 69105 is receiving some routine maintenance.
PHOTOGRAPH: I.W.COULSON/ J.W.ARMSTRONG TRUST

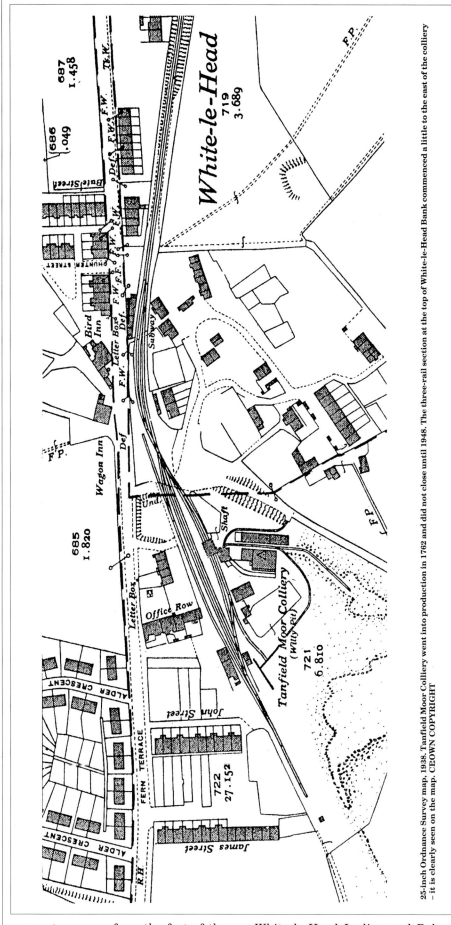

687
I.458

686
.049

Butt Street

Bird Inn

F.W. Letter Box
F.W. Def.

CHURTON STREET

F.W.F.P.
F.W. Def.

Subway

Wagon Inn

Def

F.P.

685
I.820

Letter Box

Und

Shaft

Office Row

ALDER CRESCENT

FERN TERRACE

John Street

Tanfield Moor Colliery
(Willy Pit)

721
6.810

722
27.152

James Street

ALDER CRESCENT

R.H.

White-le-Head
719
3.689

F.P.

F.P.

25-inch Ordnance Survey map, 1938. Tanfield Moor Colliery went into production in 1762 and did not close until 1948. The three-rail section at the top of White-le-Head Bank commenced a little to the east of the colliery – it is clearly seen on the map. CROWN COPYRIGHT

up empty wagons from the foot of the incline.

Each set of wagons was accompanied by a bankrider who rode up and down with the sets on the buffer beam of a wagon. It was his job to release the cable from the coupling chain at the correct time and to control the movement of wagons into the sidings.

White-le-Head Incline and Bakers Bank had three rails on their upper section, the centre rail being used by both the ascending and descending wagons. Half way down the incline the three rails diverged so as to form a conventional 'two-track' section which served as the crossing loop and which was invariably known as 'the meetings'. Below 'the meetings' the

two tracks converged to form one conventional single line.

Everyday life

The Tanfield branch, as it came to be known, settled down to regular work, though the seasonal vagaries of demand of the coal trade obviously had its effect. An NER Traffic Log sheet of *circa* 1908 reveals that, during a twelve-hour period, the two locomotives based at Bowes Bridge made a combined total of 21 trips to either Tanfield or Bakers Bank and that 66 sets of wagons were dealt with on Bakers Bank. That period was, arguably, the heyday of the Tanfield branch as, after 1918, the coal traffic started to gradually decline. Indeed, by 1945 it was about one-third of the 1907 figure.

In LNER and early BR days it was usual to find two N10s at Bowes Bridge, with an additional engine if traffic levels demanded. Apart from basic day-to-day servicing, the engines were maintained by the parent shed at Gateshead. They were changed at intervals of twenty steaming days – the outgoing engines returned to Gateshead for washouts etc and were replaced by others from Gateshead.

The substantial stone-built engine shed at Bowes Bridge was destroyed by fire in 1943 and, for some time afterwards, the engines used to stand in the open amongst the remains of the shed. However, a modern-looking brick-clad shed was erected in 1954/55.

One locomotive usually worked at Lobley Hill along Lobley Flat to Watergate Colliery. To get from Bowes Bridge shed to Lobley Hill it was usually lowered down Bakers Bank incline on the rope, usually with one or two wagons. At Lobley Hill, its duties including the sorting of loaded wagons which had to be taken down the bank to Teams (which was at the foot of the incline) and on to Redheugh; it also had to marshal the empty wagons for returning to the various collieries along the line. At the end of its shift it would work light engine up the rope worked incline to Sunniside and on to Bowes Bridge shed.

The other locomotive turn was to the various collieries in the Tanfield area, taking empties and collecting full loads. It also worked north from Bowes Bridge as far as Sunniside to feed Bakers Bank.

By the mid-1950s the coal traffic had declined so, as from September 1956, only one engine was based at Bowes Bridge. It worked a daily trip to Tanfield as well as to Lobley Hill but, as the engine now worked a nine-hour day, two sets of crew were still required. In his series of articles in the *Railway* Observer in 1958, T.E.Rounthwaite explained that the N10 left Bowes Bridge shed each morning, running bunker-first for Bakers Bank Top where it was attached to the incline rope and lowered down to Lobley Flat. It dealt with the Watergate traffic then marshalled the wagons which had to go up Bakers Bank. When all the sets of wagons had ascended, the N10 climbed the incline under its own power. It then marshalled the wagons at the top if the
continued on page 14

69109 takes water at Bowes Bridge some time in 1960. Another N10 is marshalling a group of wagons. PHOTOGRAPH: A.R.THOMPSON

The year is 1960, and 69109 is turned on the 42ft 'table at Bowes Bridge before working to Tanfield Lea. To the best of the author's knowledge 69109 was the last N10 to receive works attention. Gateshead Works having closed, it was sent to Darlington where it was repainted in the Darlington style with the number on the tank side rather than the Gateshead style whereby the number was on the bunker side (as seen in other photographs). PHOTOGRAPH: A.R.THOMPSON

Yes – it's that 1960 visit again! 69101 and 69109 have returned to Bowes Bridge shed at the end of their shift. 69109 is being coaled from the somewhat rudimentary coal stage. PHOTOGRAPH: P.J.ROBINSON

69090 passes what is now Andrews House station on the preserved Tanfield Railway with a load of coal from Tanfield Lea. PHOTOGRAPH: J.W.ARMSTRONG TRUST

Lobley Hill Incline top – a set of ascending empties has arrived on the kip and the chain is just being released. The brakesman's hut is on the left. Note the figure on the right getting the rope in the correct position. PHOTOGRAPH: J.W.ARMSTRONG TRUST

incline and proceeded with its train towards Bowes Bridge; there it was turned (a 42ft 'table had been installed in 1892) in readiness for starting its daily jaunt to Tanfield Lea. After finishing work at Tanfield Lea it returned with loaded wagons to Bowes Bridge. It was turned again before continuing to Bakers Bank. The engine and wagons descended the incline together and, after further work at Lobley Flat, the engine made its way back up the incline and brought the final load of empties to Bowes Bridge. That was it for the day.

There was one other locomotive working to be described, and indeed it was this special working which initially attracted this writer to the branch in the mid-1950s. This was the transportation of landsale coal to the depot at Tanfield Lea from, I believe, Easington Colliery –

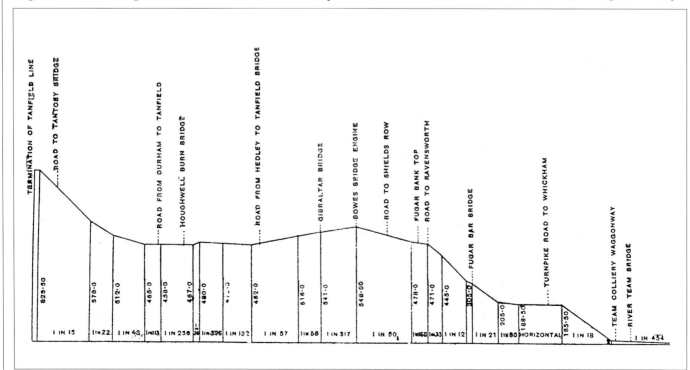

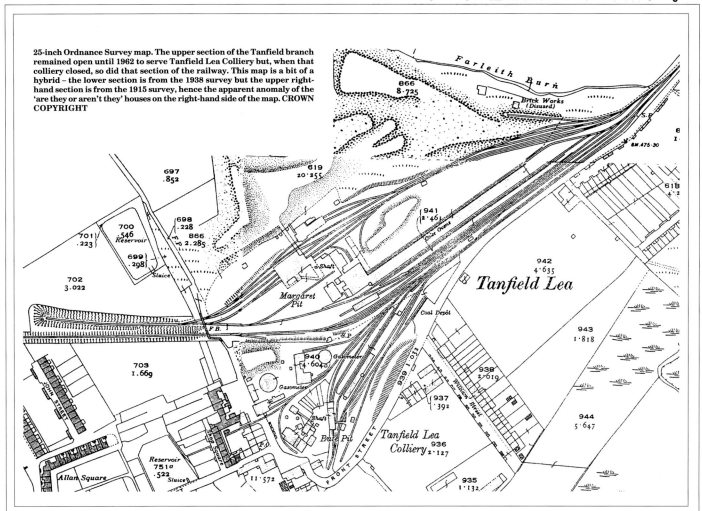

25-inch Ordnance Survey map. The upper section of the Tanfield branch remained open until 1962 to serve Tanfield Lea Colliery but, when that colliery closed, so did that section of the railway. This map is a bit of a hybrid – the lower section is from the 1938 survey but the upper right-hand section is from the 1915 survey, hence the apparent anomaly of the 'are they or aren't they' houses on the right-hand side of the map. CROWN COPYRIGHT

the coal mined at the local pits, certainly in latter days, was not of a household quality. The coal arrived at Teams and, on a Sunday morning (with overtime working of course!), two engines were despatched from Bowes Bridge, down the inclines, to push two wagons at a time up the inclines to the yard at Bowes Bridge. I believe that, in winter-time, some Saturday working also took place. The wagons were taken onwards to Tanfield Lea on a Monday morning working. The sight and sound of two N10s pushing two loaded wagons up the two inclines – Lobley Hill and Bakers Bank – was a magnificent spectacle, and was even better from the footplate! As one stretch of Bakers Bank was at a gradient of

Lobley Hill Incline with a loaded set descending. A nice job in the winter! PHOTOGRAPH: J.W.ARMSTRONG TRUST

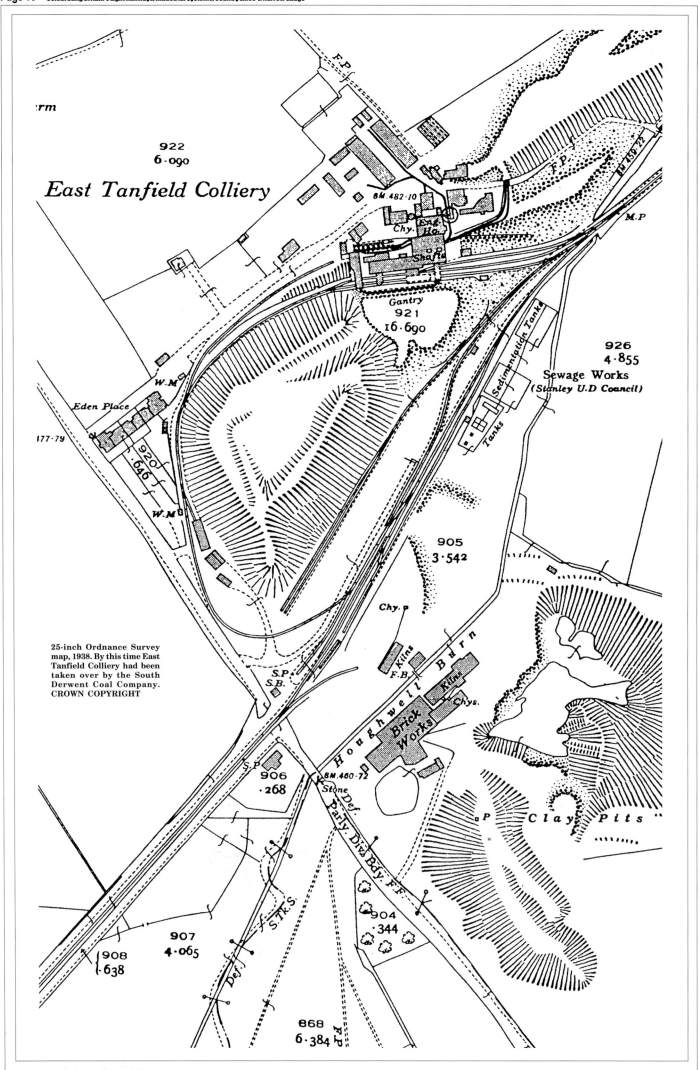

rm

922
6·090

East Tanfield Colliery

BM.482·10

Chy.
Eng.
Ho.

Shaft

Gantry
921
16·690

FP

MP

926
4·855

Sewage Works
(Stanley U.D Council)

Sedimentation Tanks

Tanks

W.M

Eden Place

177·79

920
·646

W.M

905
3·542

Chy.

25-inch Ordnance Survey
map, 1938. By this time East
Tanfield Colliery had been
taken over by the South
Derwent Coal Company.
CROWN COPYRIGHT

Kiln

F.B.

Kiln

Chys.

S.P.
S.B.

Brick Works

Houghwell Burn

S.P.

906
·268

BM.460·72

Stone

Def.

Parly. Div. Bdy. F.F.

Clay Pits

904
·344

907
4·065

Def.

S.T.K.S.

908
·638

868
6·384

FP

Bakers Bank – a set of empties descends to Lobley Hill. PHOTOGRAPH: J.W.ARMSTRONG TRUST

1 in 11, this made it even steeper than the famous Hopton Incline on the Cromford & High Peak line which is generally stated to be the steepest adhesion worked incline in the UK. Another record for the Tanfield line!

The final years

The last three N10s – Nos.69097, 69101 and 69109 – survived until April 1962. For the following four months Gateshead provided a J94 for the small amount of work which remained at Bowes Bridge. The final traffic from Watergate Colliery was, in fact, worked by a Drewry diesel from Gateshead; this locomotive was apparently kept alongside the colliery when not in use.

With the closure of Tanfield Lea Colliery – the last of the Tanfield collieries – in August 1962, much of the Tanfield Branch was rendered redundant. The section south of Watergate Colliery was therefore closed, as was the engine shed at Bowes Bridge (though the shed building remained standing for another four years or so). The final nail in the coffin was the closure of Watergate Colliery in August 1964. This deprived the remainder of the Tanfield Branch of its *raison d'être* and most of it was duly closed. A short section of line between Teams and

The bottom of Lobley Hill Incline looking to Teams with the signal box just in view in the distance. The bridge in the foreground carried the line from Gateshead to Blaydon; the second bridge carried the line from Norwood to Dunston Power Station and the third carried the line from Norwood to Dunston Staiths. The year is 1959. PHOTOGRAPH: I.H.HODGSON/ J.W.ARMSTRONG TRUST

Bakers Bank with a view of the 'meetings' where the wagons passed. This is the 1 in 11 section on the incline. PHOTOGRAPH: I.H.HODGSON/J.W.ARMSTRONG TRUST

Redheugh was kept open to serve industrial customers, but this finally succumbed in 1981.

Today

Fortunately, the closure of the Tanfield branch did not result in its total obliteration as much of it was saved for preservation. The section from Sunniside (by the A6076 road crossing) to East Tanfield has been fully relaid with new track and is now operated as a passenger-carrying line by the Tanfield Railway; that company has built stations at Sunniside, Andrews House, Causey Arch and East Tanfield. The old 1854 engine shed on the former Bowes Railway is the Tanfield Railway's headquarters and, to gain access to the branch trackbed, a new connecting link had been laid. The Tanfield is very well worth a visit. Its locomotive

Bakers Bank Top with empty wagons on the kip and the chain about to be released. The level crossing in the background carries Pennyfine Road over the railway; the crossing keeper is closing the gates to rail traffic. The year is 1959. PHOTOGRAPH: I.H.HODGSON/J.W.ARMSTRONG TRUST

The Tanfield Railway was the subject of a series of articles by T.E.Rownthwaite in the *Railway Observer* in 1958. The articles included a contemporary description of the line. With the kind permission of the RCTS (the publishers of the *Railway Observer*) we are able to reproduce, almost verbatim, that description. Remember that it refers to the 1950s...

'The best approach from Newcastle is by bus to Tantobie and thence a short walk up the village street to the moor at Whitehead.

The fast decaying Tanfield Moor Colliery buildings are close at hand at an elevation of 823ft, whilst in the immediate vicinity a narrow disused tunnel and scored and grass-grown embankments are evidence of the early tramroads in the area. Though Tanfield Moor Colliery finally ceased work in 1948 there are few signs of dismantlement and the numerous sidings and points as well as the incline are almost intact...

...Extensive views can be had from the summit of the surrounding countryside and the closed incline marks a perfectly straight course downhill to Tanfield Lea Colliery. Although the incline is grass-grown, the track is in fair condition; the three-rail section is laid with chairs of 1884 vintage on staggered 9ft sleepers.

As is common on the rest of the branch, concrete siting posts line the track at frequent intervals to guard against subsidence... A small and deserted stone signal cabin lies at the foot of the incline and, apart from duties on the telephone to the Incline Top, the signalman was also responsible for the assembly of wagons to or from the incline. A solitary signal outside the cabin guarded the approach limits of steam-hauled wagons and, in common with much of the branch signalling, the simple lever frame stands outside in the open.

The ramifications of Tanfield Lea Colliery sprawl over a considerable area near the incline foot. A short distance to the south lie the remains of the original colliery known as Bute Pit, though beyond this point there are now very few traces of the wagonway to South Moor, which closed over a century ago.

Coals leaving Tanfield Lea by rail follow the course of the original Tanfield line of the 1720s to the Tyne and, although the line falls some 500 feet, the route is by no means all downhill. Leaving the precincts of the colliery yard in a north-easterly direction, the single line commences the first stages of its long climb up to Bowes Bridge. The Tanfield East level crossing is reached within a few hundred yards and the gates are operated from the adjacent signal cabin and guarded by a pair of venerable long-armed North Eastern home signals. In 1956 one, or possibly two, freight trains only made the daily trips as far as Tanfield Lea, though by some means the aged signalman managed to stay in the box for a full day. In the cabin there are the usual block bells, though the telephone is the chief means of train advising. The signalman also relies on the distant whistling of the daily freight as a preparatory signal for opening the gates. Behind the cabin lies the very old Tanfield East Colliery...

...Just before the ascent of Causey West Bank, one of the original engine-hauled rope inclines, the Houghwell Burn, is crossed by a single span iron girder bridge bearing the name of the builders: Rayne and Burns, 1849, Newcastle. The climb to Causey is largely at 1 in 45 and at this stage the scene changes dramatically as the somewhat dreary mining aspect gives way to a delightful vista of unspoilt woods and turbulent streams with deep ravines with little or no sign of human habitation. Remains of the stables and cottages lie on the right-hand side of the line. and at the top of the bank a few stones mark the site of the old engine house and nearby a small platelayer's hut made of old stone sleepers is still in use.

For the next three-quarters of a mile the line undulates through a contortion of violent curves of 7 and 8 chains radius and a cant of four inches. The steep wall of rock on the right-hand side contrasts with the precipitous wooded slopes on the left as they fall sharply down to the Houghwell Burn far below. The track on this section has always given the permanent way men much apprehension as there is a tendency for the track to slide down to the stream! A major landslide occurred in 1912 and a new deviation had to be built further away from the river. On the left-hand side, skilfully camouflaged by a wealth of undergrowth, oak and birch saplings, lies the masterpiece of 1727 – the Causey Arch...

...Continuing northwards, the countryside opens out once more and the line is carried over the Causey Burn and valley on a substantial embankment – the first railway embankment in the world! For the next two miles the branch climbs steeply up to Bowes Bridge on gradients principally at 1 in 44/51, on what used to be the Causey East rope-hauled incline. Some distance up the bank lies Causey level crossing, together with a gate house protected by the familiar pair of home signals and outside lever frame.

Nearing the top of Causey East Bank the line enters a cutting which gradually widens out at the approaches to Bowes Bridge shed and yard. The cutting is bisected by the NCB colliery line from Marley Hill to the coast at Jarrow, better known in modern times as the Bowes Railway, and the two lines cross each other on a very blind right-angle crossing. A corner of the cutting has been carved out for the site of the small brick and timber signal cabin, and although at the present time the NCB have the right of way, the box is manned each morning by BR staff to signal the passage of the daily freight train to and from Tanfield.

The adjacent Marley Hill Colliery was one of the earliest in the district and, after a period of disuse, it was re-established in 1840 by John Bowes & Partners who in turn linked up their other collieries to the east and west by their own railway system. The coals which formerly used the Tanfield line were then transferred to the Bowes line on its completion in 1854, and have been so conveyed up to the present time. However, pit props for Marley Hill are still brought in over the Tanfield line.

A group of reception sidings, a neat brick brakesman's cabin and other buildings for bank riders and stores announce the arrival at the head of Bakers Bank Incline – the first of the self acting inclines. The incline is one mile in length. An additional safety hitch is in force here, and the brake and binding wheels lie concealed just beneath ground level opposite the brake hut. Train loads of full wagons arriving from Bowes Bridge are split up into sets of three or four wagons according to their capacity, and providing similar empties are available at the incline foot, the silent and effortless process of the self acting incline is put into motion. The top and bottom of the incline are in touch with each other by block bell and telephone. The optimum tonnage is 93 tons loaded down and 55 tons of empties up and a travelling speed of 12-16mph.

The operation of Bakers Bank is aggravated by a level crossing virtually at the summit and the greatest care has to be taken with the control of road traffic. Although Bakers Bank Incline has a well nigh straight descent, the line curves quite sharply on the single track section near the bottom. Immediately below the bottom set of loop points the line passes through a very narrow road bridge carrying the main road to Newcastle, and this bridge was the scene of a serious accident in 1939. Wagons were derailed and, today, the facing stones of the bridge bear the scars of the impact and the splashes from a fractured tar wagon.

At the foot of the bank the line fans out into a series of long sidings, together with an office and water column, and for the next half-mile to the head of Lobley Hill Incline the ground is relatively level. A branch to the prosperous and relatively modern Watergate Colliery strikes off from the east side of Lobley Flat, and about 700 tons of coal a dyay are brought out of the colliery for the final descent to the Tyne.

Immediately prior to reaching the Lobley Hill Incline top, and the ancillary buildings and sidings, the branch is crossed by the Whickham-Newcastle Road and the level crossing is guarded by a signal cabin. At this point the River Tyne, which so far has been elusive, suddenly comes into full view some 200 feet below, and on a clear day an excellent panorama into Northumberland is afforded.

The descent of the 1,000-yard Lobley Hill Incline is made principally at 1 in 16, curving down towards the Tyne. Starting its course amidst a welter of new housing, the incline terminates amongst a network of industrial undertakings. Oddly enough the actual foot of the incline lies beneath two railway bridges carrying the Team branch to Dunston. Beyond the incline foot the Tanfield branch crosses what used to be the Pelaw Main route to the Tyne. Although the crossing has been removed, a connection has recently been laid to the Tanfield line. Nearby are the gas works and coke ovens which today are the final destination of most of the railborne coal from the Tanfield and Wategate collieries, though the branch does reach the bank of the Tyne and, after passing the site of the original shipping staiths, it proceeds along the wharves to the shadow of the Redheugh bridge. The climb from this point up to Gateshead was a formidable one, mainly at 1 in 22 and 1 in 37, and although it was originally a rope worked incline it succumbed to the locomotive many years ago'.

Collieries

Over the years several collieries have been served by the Tanfield branch though, by the time the NCB came into existence in 1947, just four remained. From the south-west these were:

Tanfield Moor: This was a very old concern which went into production as far back as 1762. Initially owned by the Earl of Kerry, it then passed to James Joicey & Co which, as a result of amalgamations, eventually became Lambton Hetton & Joicey Collieries. Tanfield Moor was, in effect, a combination of numerous small pits which, over the years, included Conquest, Mount and Willy pits. In the late 1890s Tanfield Moor employed some 365 people – 300 underground and 65 on the surface. The average annual output in the 1890s was 130,000 tons, but by 1947 the figure was just 27,000 tons. An LNER document dated 1927 states that the colliery was 'now closed and the incline is not being used', but we have found no evidence to support this. If there *was* a closure in the 1920s, it could have been only a temporary one. Indeed, it is on record that the colliery closed in October 1948 and the incline down to Tanfield Lea was then taken out of use. Unlike most collieries in the area Tanfield Moor did not have its own shunting locomotive; to the best of our knowledge the wagons to and from the colliery were manoeuvred by winches.

Tanfield Lea: Tanfield Lea was sunk by the Marquis of Bute in 1829 and was acquired by James Joicey in 1847. It comprised four pits: Ann, Bute, Margaret and Wind pit. At its peak in 1914 it had a staff of 1,469 – 1,229 underground and 240 on the surface. In the 1890s it yielded an average of 305,000 tons per annum while in 1947 (the first year of the NCB's existence) the output was 120,500 tons. Closure came on 25 August 1962.

Railway operations at the colliery seem to have been undertaken by the NER until *circa* 1900 when the colliery acquired its own locomotive. In NCB days the colliery locomotives were:
• R.W.Hawthorn 0-6-0ST (W/No.1430 of 1868) – transferred to Morrison Busty Colliery in 1947
• Hawthorn Leslie 0-4-0ST EDEN (W/No.2481 of 1900) – shared its time between Tanfield Lea and Marley Hill collieries until the closure of Tanfield Lea in August 1962, when it was permanently transferred to Marley Hill
• Kerr Stuart 0-4-0ST (W/No.4030 of 1919) – shared its time between Tanfield Lea, East Tanfield and Marley Hill until the closure of Tanfield Lea in August 1962, when it was permanently transferred to Marley Hill Colliery
• Barclay 0-4-0ST (W/No.2274 of 1949) – came to Tanfield Lea in October 1957; remained (albeit not continuously) until November 1959 when it returned to Marley Hill Colliery.

East Tanfield: This colliery was sunk by James Joicey in 1844 but is reported to have been closed in 1908. It was revived under the new ownership of the East Tanfield Colliery Company in 1917 and was sold to the South Derwent Coal Co in 1930. The colliery's busiest period was during and immediately after World War II when almost 900 people were employed there – over 700 underground, the remainder on the surface. The output in 1947 was 161,500 tons. During the 1955 rail strike much of the colliery's output went by road; the railway failed to recover the traffic and, from 1958, all traffic went by road. However, that situation did not prevail for too long as the colliery closed on 9 January 1961.

The colliery locos in NCB days were:
• Barclay 0-4-0ST STANLEY No.1 (W/No.1659 of 1920) – spent five months at Marley Hill colliery in 1950; returned to East Tanfield but was permanently transferred to Marley Hill in July 1954
• 0-4-0ST STANLEY No.2 (built by Hudswell Clarke c.1881 but rebuilt by Lingford Gardiner of Bishop Auckland in 1914) – apparently remained at East Tanfield after the cessation of rail traffic and scrapped in June 1962
• Kerr Stuart 0-4-0ST (W/No.4030 of 1919) – had a few months here in 1950 and returned for a few weeks in February/March 1953
• Barclay 0-4-0ST (W/No.2274 of 1949) – was here from October 1954 to October 1956 and again from November 1957 until the cessation of rail traffic in April 1958 when it returned to Tanfield Lea Colliery.

Watergate: Watergate Colliery was opened in 1926 by Priestman Collieries Ltd. In the late 1940s it yielded an average of 200,000 tons per annum and had a staff of over 700, of whom 580 worked underground. The greatest number of staff was in 1960 – 750 underground and 170 on the surface. Watergate remained in production until 20 August 1964, by which time it had become the last working colliery served by the Tanfield branch.

The colliery locos in NCB days were:
• Hudswell Clarke 0-4-0ST WALDRIDGE No.2 (W/No.674 of 1903, rebuilt by Hawthorn Leslie in 1925) – transferred to Lilley Drift c.1950
• Hawthorn Leslie 0-4-0ST CLAUDE (W/No.2349 of 1896) – ex-Blaydon Burn Colliery 1950; transferred to Ouston 'E' Colliery in 1959
• Ex-NER Y7 class 0-4-0T 1308 (built at Gateshead 1891) – ex-Ravensworth Ann Colliery 1954; returned there later that year
• Ex-NER Y7 class 0-4-0T 1310 (built at Gateshead 1891) – ex-Ravensworth Ann Colliery 1959; to Middleton Railway for preservation, June 1965.

..........ooooo000ooooo..........

Mention should also be made of Marley Hill Colliery. This colliery originally despatched coal via the Tanfield branch but, with the opening of the Pontop & Jarrow line (later known as the Bowes Railway) in 1854 its coal was diverted to the new line. However, the connections to the Tanfield branch were retained until the closure of the line.

fleet includes the greatest number of industrial locomotives at any one site anywhere in England, the emphasis being on Tyneside-built locomotives or those which worked in the north-east. The section from Tanfield Moor to Tanfield Lea is now a walkway and the section from Sunniside to Teams Crossing is now a footpath, but the old trackbed from Tanfield Lea to East Tanfield has disappeared under a road and industrial units.

Acknowledgements: *Reference was made to* The North Eastern Railway – its rise and development *by W.W.Tomlinson (1914), articles by T.E.Rounthwaite in various issues of the* Railway Observer *(1958),* 1725 Onwards *(the guide book of the Tanfield Railway),* Carrying Coals to Dunston *by E.Manns (Oakwood Press, 2000) and to* Industrial Locomotives of County Durham *(Industrial Railway Society, 1977). Assistance was kindly provided by the staff of Durham Mining Museum (information on various collieries on the line) and by D.G.Charlton (various notes, articles and information, some written by the late L.G.Charlton).*

The verbatim extracts from the Railway Observer *articles have been reproduced by the kind permission of the Railway Correspondence & Travel Society. To find out more about the RCTS – the UK's leading railway enthusiasts society – visit their website at www.rcts.org.uk*

Top right. **It's the end of the shift and 69100 comes up Bakers Bank under its own steam after working at Lobley Hill. Note the three-rail section – the centre rail was 'common' for ascending and descending wagons (no – *not* simultaneously!)   PHOTOGRAPH: J.W.ARMSTRONG TRUST**

Photo right. **An N10 descends Bakers Bank with empty wagons some time during 1959. In the background is Watergate Colliery. PHOTOGRAPH: I.H.HODGSON/J.W.ARMSTRONG TRUST**

69100 shunts at the top of Lobley Hill. A bus going in the Gateshead direction waits for it to clear the level crossing. This crossing is of interest as the original 'Whickham Way' of *circa* 1620 crossed the road here. The 'Whickham Way' became part of the Tanfield Waggonway and survived until 1964, so coal traffic crossed the Whickham highway at this point for more than 340 years! PHOTOGRAPH: J.W.ARMSTRONG TRUST

Teams Crossing at the foot of Lobley Hill Incline in the 1920s. Norwood Colliery, which was served by the Pelaw Main Colliery line is on the right. We are looking north in the direction of Newcastle. PHOTOGRAPH: L.G.CHARLTON

The author's favourite spectacle on the Tanfield line was the special landsale coal working on Sundays (and sometimes also on Saturdays during the winter). This involved two N10s – here they tackle the 1 in 11 section of Bakers Bank with the two wagons of landsale coal in 1959. PHOTOGRAPH: A.R.THOMPSON

The 'landsale train' at Teams, at the bottom of Lobley Hill Incline, in 1960. In the background is Redheugh Gas Works. PHOTOGRAPH: I.H.HODGSON/J.W.ARMSTRONG TRUST

FOURUM – NCB STEAM IN THE 1970s
Photographs by Steve Leyland

Take yourself back to 1970. It is more than two years since the very last ordinary steam working on BR, but steam was still to be found at many industrial sites throughout Britain. The NCB, in particular, was still a prolific user of steam in 1970 – this was the scene at Brynlliw Colliery at Grovesend, five miles or so to the north-west of Swansea, on 7 September 1970. One of the colliery's Peckett 0-6-0STs heads a rake of empties from the exchange sidings to the colliery. We say 'one of the colliery Pecketts' as, at the time, Brynlliw had three Pecketts. However, we reckon this is a B3 type and, if that is correct, it is W/ No.2114 of 1952 which remained at the colliery until it closed in 1983.

A few miles to the north-east of Brynlliw Colliery was Graig Merthyr Colliery where, on 7 September 1970, Barclay 0-4-0ST GRAIG MERTHYR was photographed at the weighbridge. This engine had been built in 1920 for the colliery's original owners, the Graigola Merthyr Company, and remained on site until 1973 when it was scrapped.

Moving almost thirty miles to the east, Wern Tawr Colliery near Pencoed, four miles or so to the east of Bridgend, was served by a ¹/₂-mile branch line from the main WR line near Llanharan. In the late 1960s and early 1970s there were usually two or three engines at the colliery, one of which was Avonside 0-6-0ST TON PHILLIP which took its name from Ton Phillip Colliery at Cefn Cribbwr where it had been delivered new in 1920. When photographed at Wern Tawr on 5 July 1971 it was laid up awaiting repair, its duties being performed instead by ex-BR 204hp diesel D2244. One interesting aspect of this scene is what appears to be a spare tubeplate above the wagon on the left.

And now moving north to the valleys... Barclay 0-6-0T No.1 (W/No.2340 of 1953) was photographed near the level crossing on the Merthyr Vale Colliery system on 7 July 1971. This engine had gone new to the NCB's railway system at Aberaman and had come to Merthyr Vale in 1965. It had a brief stint at Mardy Colliery in 1966/67 but returned to Merthyr Vale and saw out its days there, being scrapped in the summer of 1975.

LONDON TRANSPORT SERVICE LOCOMOTIVES – pre-Pannier days
by Frank Goudie (with additional material by I.C.Coleford)

Ex-Metropolitan Peckett 0-6-0ST L53 at Neasden, 18 October 1958. Inside the shed is 'E' class 0-4-4T L48 which, although retained mainly for departmental duties, had originally been one of the Met's front line of passenger motive power. PHOTOGRAPH: THE TRANSPORT TREASURY

Various issues of *Railway Bylines* magazine have referred to Metropolitan and District Railway 'main line' steam locomotives which finished up in London Transport service stock for departmental duties – the handful of Beyer Peacock 4-4-0Ts, four of the 'E' class 0-4-4Ts and the 'F' class 0-6-2Ts. Those locomotives were ousted in the 1950s/60s by ex-WR Pannier Tanks, and these, too, have featured in *Bylines* from time to time. But what of the steam locomotives which were purchased by the Metropolitan, the District and other 'underground' companies *specifically* for departmental duties? This category encompasses seven locomotives from four different companies.

Metropolitan Railway
In 1880 the Metropolitan's extension line had reached Harrow-on-the-Hill and an important goods yard was opened there. In October of that same year a junction with the Midland Railway was established at Finchley Road, with a goods yard for the exchange of traffic between the two companies. As the century drew to a close the yards at Harrow and Finchley Road were handling an ever-increasing amount of goods traffic and the Metropolitan Railway considered that it would be advantageous to

purchase a locomotive specifically for shunting at Harrow yard.

To fill that requirement, early in 1897 an order was placed with Peckett & Sons of Bristol for one of their standard 'X' class 0-6-0STs. Costing £1,390, the locomotive was delivered in March 1897. As Peckett's Works No.664, it was designated Metropolitan Railway No.101. It was a typically handsome machine, having a copper-capped flared chimney, two spring-balance Salter safety valves on the dome and rectangular sandboxes on the footplate in front of the leading wheels. The new locomtive was described in *The Locomotive Magazine* in July 1897: '…*it is fitted with both steam and hand brake operating cast iron blocks on all the wheels, and it is an exceptional instance on the Metropolitan Railway of an engine not provided with condensing apparatus*'. The lack of condensing apparatus wasn't a problem, of course, as the locomotive was intended for yard shunting, not for subterranean duties. Interestingly, though, the report in *The Locomotive* did not refer to the locomotive being used on yard shunting; it stated that it was used for shunting at the Metropolitan Railway's workshops at Neasden.

Shortly after it entered service No.101 was used for hauling spoil trains during the construction of the Great Central's

approach to Marylebone, a huge quantity of spoil having been excavated from the tunnel under Lords cricket ground at St.John's Wood. No.101 proved to be a useful acquisition so a second, almost identical, engine was purchased from Peckett & Sons in November 1899 at a cost of £1,595. This was Peckett's Works No.823 – it became Metropolitan No.102.

The Metropolitan's two Pecketts sported the company's standard dark red livery, fully lined out in black and yellow with METROPOLITAN RAILWAY in an oval scroll surrounding the engine number on the saddle tank; in later years this was changed to the single word METROPOLITAN carried on the tank with the engine number high up on the cab side. It seems that the Pecketts were not given a class letter by the Metropolitan, though a photograph does exist of No.101 with the letter 'B' painted below its running number. This is something of a mystery as the Met already had a 'B' class – these were the second generation of the famous Beyer Peacock 4-4-0Ts.

No.101 received general overhauls in 1911 and 1921, the latter including the fitting of a new copper firebox and new cylinders. No.102 was fitted with new cylinders in 1906, was fitted with a Jones patent blastpipe in 1920 and had a

SUMMARY OF LOCOMOTIVES

	Peckett 0-6-0STs L53, L54	Hunslet 0-6-0Ts	Kerr Stuart 0-4-2ST L34	Hunslet 0-6-0Ts L30, L31
Original owner	Metropolitan Railway	Central London Ry.	City & South London Ry.	District Railway
Cylinders:	16" x 22" (i)	14" x 18" (i)	9" x 15" (o)	16" x 24" (o)
Heating surfaces – firebox:		51 sq.ft.		74 sq.ft.
– tubes:		511 sq.ft.		778 sq.ft.
TOTAL:	712 sq.ft.	562 sq.ft.		852 sq.ft.
Grate area:	13.25 sq.ft.	8.5 sq.ft.		14.5 sq,ft,
Boiler pressure:	140 psi	160 psi	160 psi	200 psi
Tractive effort (@ 85%):	14,560 lbs	10,855 lbs	6,500 lbs	18,432 lbs
Haulage capability on level*:	1,180 tons	570 tons		980 tons
Coupled wheels:	3' 10"	3' 3"	2' 6"	4' 2"
Trailing wheels:	-	-		-
Wheelbase:	11' 0"	8' 6"		13' 0"
Height from rail level:	12' 1"	9' 4½"	9' 6"	12' 3"
Extreme width:	8' 6"	8' 3½"		8' 10¼"
Total length over buffers:	28' 5"	23' 3¼"		
Water capacity:	1,160 galls	250 galls	270 galls	1,200 galls
Coal capacity:	1 ton 0 cwt	9 cwt	15 cwt	1 ton 10 cwt
Oil capacity:	-	50 galls	-	-
Weight (full):	39 tons 0 cwt	31 tons 17 cwt	14 tons 0 cwt	44 tons 6½ cwt
Max. axle weight:		11 tons 7 cwt		14 tons 15½ cwt

* Maker's figures

'general' in 1923. Otherwise, apart from livery changes, the two engines remained virtually unaltered throughout their lives.

In 1925 No.102 had a spell on hire to the District Railway, deputising for the latter company's No.33, a Beyer Peacock 4-4-0T which was about to be withdrawn. The District's other surviving 4-4-0T, No.34, was undergoing a protracted repair at the time, hence the need to hire a replacement. The District asked the Met if it could purchase both of the Pecketts or, alternatively, two of the Met's remaining 4-4-0Ts (at that time the Met still had eleven 4-4-0Ts of its own) but, in the event, the Met retained the two Pecketts and sold one of its 4-4-0Ts to the District for £300. This was Met No.22 which became District No.35 and survived until 1931.

It seems likely that the Pecketts were used to take away the remains of Sir Edward Watkin's ill-fated tower at Wembley Park when it was dismantled in 1906. The engines were also used on the daily goods train from Neasden to Willesden Green. Otherwise, their duties were never particularly arduous nor glamorous. Under the terms of the Metropolitan & Great Central Joint Railways agreement the Met and the GCR (later LNER) shared the shunting duties at Harrow goods yard for alternative five-year periods and, as this reduced the Pecketts' spheres of activity, it was far from unusual to find one or other of the pair laid up. Indeed, there is a well-known photograph of No.102 in store at Neasden in 1924 looking neglected and far from the impeccable condition in which

Metropolitan locomotives were usually kept.

Nos.101 and 102 passed to the London Passenger Transport Board when it took over the Metropolitan Railway in July 1933. In 1937 they were renumbered L53 and L54 respectively in London Transport service stock. Under LT auspices they were subjected to the requisite livery changes; the words LONDON TRANSPORT replaced the Metropolitan name on the saddle tanks and, when the 1937 renumbering took place, L54 was initially repainted in the LT style, but in the old Metropolitan dark red. That, however, was later replaced by LT dark red.

From 1937 until the 1950s both of the Pecketts were usually employed at Neasden Yard, their duties there including shunting at the power station where they fed wagons of coal into the coal hoists and removed wagons of ash and slurry. In later years L54 was transferred to Lillie Bridge. L53 remained at Neasden, but by 1960 there was not enough work to keep it busy there and, as it was no longer permitted on the 'main line', it was withdrawn. It was cut up during November 1960. The escapee at Lillie Bridge, L54, also saw its workload dwindle and, consequently, it was withdrawn in September 1961. It was cut up the following February.

Central London Railway

The Central London Railway was one of the electric 'tube' companies which became part of the 'Underground Group' in 1913 and, eventually, part of London Transport. The CLR's contribution to the underground map was a significant part

L53 in its original guise as Metroplitan No.101 – this picture was taken at Neasden (where else?) on 12 May 1934. PHOTOGRAPH: H.C.CASSERLEY

Ex-Metropolitan No.102 in its recently acquired London Transport livery at Neasden on 11 July 1935. PHOTOGRAPH: H.C.CASSERLEY

of what became the Central Line. In 1899 – while the CLR was equipping its soon-to-be-opened line between Shepherds Bush and Bank – the company purchased two specially-designed 0-6-0Ts from the Hunslet Engine Co. Carrying Works Nos.695 and 696, the first was delivered in July 1899 and the second the following month.

They were 'cut down' engines with low roofs to their cabs, thereby enabling them to be used in the CLR's tunnels. The locomotives could operate as coal burners, a conventional grate, a small bunker and a small 250-gallon tank being fitted, but they could also operate as oil-burners, for which they were fitted with Holden's patent oil-burning equipment and a

bunker tank for 50 gallons of oil. When operating as oil-burners they could be worked by a crew of one, a fireman not being required. Another of their distinctive features was the twin sets of buffers – a pair of conventional buffers for ordinary shunting work and a pair of smaller buffers for use with the CLR's 'tube' rolling stock.

Although LT service locos were frequently photographed at their depots, they weren't often photographed while 'out on the road' so to speak. This rarity is Peckett L53 on what appears to be an ordinary goods working at Willesden Green on 1 September 1954. PHOTOGRAPH: F.W.GOUDIE

The maker's official portrait of Central London Railway No.1. As noted in the text the engine could operate as a coal-burner or an oil-burner; the hefty side tanks were not for injector water, but for condensing purposes. An article in the 17 November 1899 edition of *The Engineer* stated that the engine: '...*is to be capable of hauling from the deep level tunnels a train of seven bogie coaches – weighing in all about 100 tons – up a straight gradient of 1 in 50 for a length of 350 yards, followed by a 1 in 37 for 300 yards, and then by 200 yards of 1 in 40 which is on a curve of 300ft radius. It must also be able to traverse curves of 150ft radius and go through the loading gauge of the Central London Railway*'. **PHOTOGRAPH: COURTESY DON TOWNSLEY**

They were fitted with condensing apparatus and, in conjunction with this, had full-length side tanks which could store 1,000 gallons of water. That said, in his definitive tome *The Hunslet Engine Works,* author Don Townsley explains that the word 'condensing' should be used somewhat loosely as, although the exhaust (smoke plus steam) was passed through the water in the side tanks and did reduce the eventual emission of airborne solids, it did not convert *all* the exhaust to water, so the more correct terminology these days would be 'exhaust gas conditioning' or 'scrubbing'.

The purchase of the locomotives almost a year before the line was opened reflected the fact that they were intended to be used during the equipping of the line. After the public opening of the line in July 1900 the locomotives were used mainly on shunting duties at Wood Lane Power Station which was served by sidings off the joint GWR/LNW West London line, but they were also used on works trains and, when necessary, rescue work.

By the early 1920s the two locomotives were based at Lillie Bridge but it seems that, by this time, they were seldom used. In 1924 they were sold to the well-known dealers, J.F.Wake of Darlington. Wake's offered the locomotives for resale, but there were no takers so the engines remained in the yard and became increasingly derelict. In 1926 or thereabouts a locomotive was required at Wake's slag and tarmacadam works at Port Clarence, County Durham, so Wake's cannibalised the two ex-CLR engines to

provide enough parts to build one serviceable one. The resultant engine – which bore Wakes' plate 2805 – remained at the Port Clarence works for several years, though by the mid-1940s it was little, if ever, used. It finally departed in September 1948 when it was sold for scrap to J.Shaw Ltd of Hartlepool.

City & South London Railway

The City & South London Railway was another of the pioneering electric 'tube' companies, its contribution to the underground map being a considerable part of what became the Northern Line. The C&SL became part of the 'Underground Group' in 1913 and was therefore required to enlarge its tunnels to the standard diameter of 11ft 8 ¼in, but it was 1922 before this work was put in hand. To help with the work the C&SL purchased a little Kerr Stuart 'Brazil' class 0-4-2ST (W/No.4215). This engine's height of just 9ft 6in enabled it to work in the tunnels; it originally had just a rudimentary roof over the footplate but, in later years, it was fitted with a back sheet and a curving roof which offered a little more protection against the elements.

The Kerr Stuart was later used during the construction of the C&SL's extension from Stockwell to Morden. This job was put in hand in 1924 and was completed in September 1926. In 1930 the locomotive was renumbered L34 and was later taken into London Transport service stock. In LT days it was used on various construction jobs including the Piccadilly

extension to Cockfosters and the eastern extension of the Central Line to Leytonstone. It is a little unclear whether the locomotive was withdrawn from service after the completion of the Central Line extension in May 1947 or whether it was retained for use on the electrification through to Epping and then withdrawn.

District Railway

Earlier, mention was made of the District Railway's purchase of a 4-4-0T from the Metropolitan Railway in 1925. This meant that the District had two Beyer Peacocks, Nos.34 and 35, to look after shunting duties at Lillie Bridge depot and ballast train working. However, No.35 was withdrawn in 1931 and, as No.34 was also considered to be coming towards the end of its life, the District bought replacements for both.

The replacements were purchased new from the Hunslet Engine Company of Leeds. As W/Nos.1674 and 1675, they were dispatched by the makers on 9 February 1931. They were smart, very efficient-looking 0-6-0Ts with outside cylinders and Walschaerts valve gear; to adhere to the District's loading gauge they were built to a width of 8ft 10 ¼in and a maximum height of 12ft 3in. They were designated L30 and L31 – the first District or Metropolitan steam locomotives to have the 'L' prefix. When delivered they were painted olive green with the word UNDERGROUND and the running number on the tank sides. When taken over by London Transport they retained their numbers but were routinely repainted in LT lined red with LONDON TRANSPORT lettering.

The two Hunslets were based at Lillie Bridge. Their principal duties there were yard shunting, but they were also used on stores trains to and from Acton Works and Ealing Common Depot, on ballast trains and, during the winter, for brushing snow off icy conductor rails. Their duties very occasionally took them to unexpected locations; for example, on 1 October 1950 L30, which was being used on bridge renewal work between Parsons Green and Putney Bridge, was observed collecting wagons at Wimbledon sorting sidings.

By early 1963 L31 had been transferred to Neasden. In the severe January of that year it made several trips to Amersham and Chesham to brush ice from the rails. L30 and L31 were both kept active for duties in connection with the Metropolitan's Centenary Exhibition at Neasden in May 1963 but they were withdrawn shortly afterwards, their regular duties being taken over by Pannier Tanks.

The City & South London Railway's Kerr Stuart 0-4-2ST is seen here more or less in its original guise with a very basic roof and an open-backed footplate. This picture was taken at Lillie Bridge on 28 May 1931. PHOTOGRAPH: H.C.CASSERLEY

Contributors' note: Thanks to Mr. Don Townsley for additional information about the District Railway's and the Central London Railway's Hunslet locomotives. Thanks also to Mr. Russell Wear of the Industrial Locomotive Society; for details of the ILS send an s.a.e. to the Membership Secretary, 24 Butterfield Road, Over Hulton, Bolton BL5 1DU or visit their website at www.industrial-loco.org.uk

Seen here as London Transport L34 and with somewhat better protection for the crew, the ex-City & South London Kerr Stuart had a number of unusual features including round-section rods and box-like sandboxes near the cylinders and behind the saddle tank. PHOTOGRAPH: ERIC ASHTON COLLECTION

The District Railway's Hunslet 0-6-0T L30 is seen at Lillie Bridge on 28 May 1931 – immediately after delivery. Its livery is unlined chocolate brown. PHOTOGRAPH: H.C.CASSERLEY

Hunslet 0-6-0T L31 at Lillie Bridge depot some time in the 1950s. Its livery was the same maroon as that used on surviving Metropolitan engines. PHOTOGRAPH: G.CLARKE

DERWENT VALLEY STATIONS – a case of commendable maintenance
Photographs by F.W.Shuttleworth; all taken on 11 April 1955

The Derwent Valley Light Railway, which was intended primarily to serve growers in the agricultural area between York and Cliff Common, was opened to goods and livestock traffic on 29 October 1912, but it was 21 July the following year before it opened to passengers. Passenger traffic ceased as early as August 1926 but the line remained open to goods traffic for many more years. Indeed, it remained open throughout until 1964 and the very last section did not close until 1981. Although it had been authorised as a *bona fide* light railway the Derwent Valley had such 'main line' luxuries as gated level crossings, lineside fencing and 'proper' stations with full-size platforms. There were no less than eleven stations along the 16-mile route. This is Dunnington for Kexby (to give it its full title from its passenger days). In the 1950s Dunnington generated a respectable amount of goods traffic; most of it was from Messrs Yorkshire Grain Driers who, in later years, even had their own diesel locomotive. Here we are looking towards York.

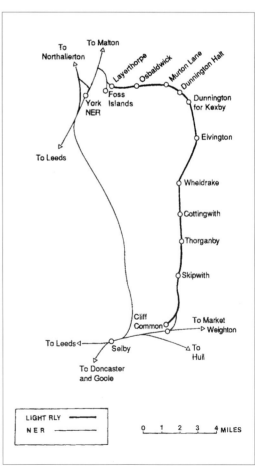

The first station along the line from York was Osbaldwick. In common with all the other intermediate stations along the line, the platform was 200ft in length and 3ft high. When this picture was taken in 1955 the station and yard were used by Messrs.W.& J.Glossop, a firm of tar distillers. In the 1960s there was also a pre-mix concrete plant in the station yard. This view also looks towards York.

Dunnington was one of two halts on the line (the other was West Cottingwith) but, despite the railway's humble status, the halts had 'proper' station buildings similar to, but slightly smaller than, those at the other stations. Once again we are looking towards York.

Although the Derwent Valley had lost its scheduled passenger services way back in 1926, the company kept its stations and rented out the buildings. In its later years, the Derwent Valley Railway Company was doing almost as well as a property company as it was as a railway company. This is Elvington station. Here we see further evidence that, despite the loss of the passenger traffic, the company kept the stations in very good order.

Above. Wheldrake station, looking towards Selby. This was another station which generated a fair amount of goods traffic in post-war years, in this case principally from a Ministry of Agriculture buffer depot which was used for the storage of sugar. The connections for the sidings (which are out of view here) were worked from small ground frames which were originally locked by the key staff, but following a change of working hours in 1924 (partly a consequence of the introduction of the eight-hour day) the line was divided into four sections under an arrangement somewhat like the train staff and ticket. The sections were York-Dunnington, Dunnington-Wheldrake, Wheldrake-Skipwith and Skipwith-Cliff Common, so Wheldrake found itself to be a 'staff' station.

Top right. Despite the similarity of style of the Derwent Valley station buildings, probably the nearest one got to actual duplication was at Wheldrake and Thorganby. York is to the left and Selby to the right.

Right. Skipwith station – or Skipwith & North Duffield, to give it its full title – was another of the stations which found itself at the end of a staff section as a result of the revised working arrangements of 1924. Given that this station – and, come to that, the other stations along the line as well – was on an out-of-the-way light railway and had never been intended to cope with huge numbers of passengers (as we have seen, the railway had catered for fare-paying passengers for only 13 years), the platform buildings were rather more substantial than those on many 'ordinary' branch lines in other parts of the country. And that's not to mention the standard of maintenance...

FOURUM — RETURN TO SOUTHWELL
Photographs by Keith Vernon

In *Bylines 7:9* (August 2002) we looked at the Rolleston Junction-Southwell push-pulls. These workings were a photographer's delight, so we make no apologies for featuring them again here. We kick off with a view of ex-Midland 0-4-4T 58065 and the push-pull coach standing outside the small shed at Southwell. It is thought that this and the other photographs were taken in 1958.

The driving end of the ex-Midland auto trailer at Southwell. We don't have the number of this vehicle to hand, but it could be M24400 which was in regular use on the line in 1957/58.

58085 is ready to depart from Southwell with the push-pull to Rolleston Junction. The lines beyond the station (in the distance) continue to Mansfield, but the passenger services beyond Southwell had been discontinued in 1929. As for our 58085, the usual practice in 1958 was for it to work the morning trains and to be relieved by class-mate 58065 at midday. 58085 went on to become one of the very last survivors of the class, being withdrawn in April 1959.

A splendid study of the bracket signals and some of the other platform fittings and furniture at Southwell. Lovely!

THE BROAD AND THE NARROW –
the Guinness brewery (Dublin) and its railways by Ian P.Peaty

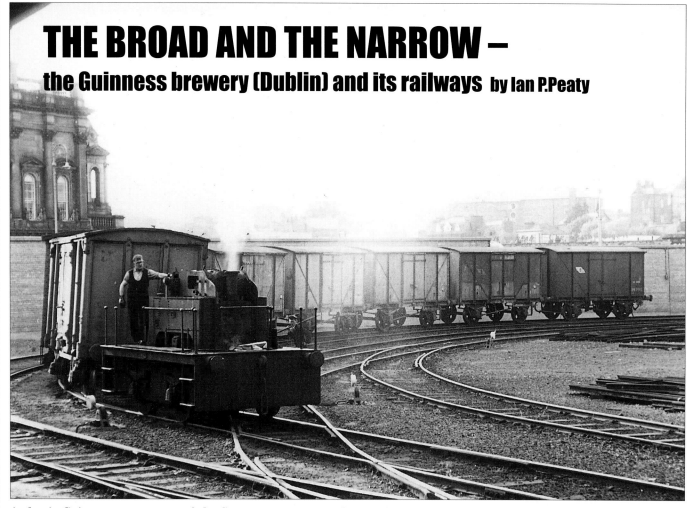

A classic Guinness scene – one of the Spence narrow gauge locomotives mounted on a broad gauge 'haulage wagon' hauls a rake of wagons round the curve just inside the boundary wall towards the loading bank. This picture is believed to have been taken in 1965. The edifice in the background is the imposing frontage of the old GS&WR Kingsbridge passenger station.
PHOTOGRAPH: AUTHOR'S COLLECTION

In 1670 Giles Mee, the Lord Mayor of Dublin, sold his small brewery at St.James's Gate to Alderman Sir Mark Rainsford. The brewery passed to Sir Mark's son in 1709, but in 1759 the premises were acquired by one Arthur Guinness. Our Mr.Guinness had been left £100 by his late godfather, the Archbishop of Cashel, and had gained experience of brewing at a small brewery in Leixlip in County Kildare, but it was nevertheless a very big step for the 31-year-old to go off for the big city of Dublin to set up his own business.

When Arthur Guinness acquired the St.James's Gate brewery the premises were very run down and the deal included a copper, a kieve, a mill, two malt houses, stables for twelve horses and a loft for 200 tons of hay. The lease was for 9,000(!) years and the original rent was just £45 p.a. The water supply for Arthur Guinness's brewery came by pipeline from the hills ten miles to the west. A supply of good quality water is, of course, essential for brewing, and the importance of the water supply for Arthur Guinness's brewery is evidenced by a well-known story... Following a dispute about water rights in 1775, Dublin Corporation officials turned up at the brewery to cut off the supply. The normally reserved and peaceable Arthur Guinness grabbed a pickaxe from one of the men and proclaimed that he was prepared to

'defend his rights by force of arms'. Fortunately, force proved unnecessary and Arthur secured his water rights by more conventional means.

As for the brewery's products, back in the early 1720s brewers in far-away London were producing a dark beer that was to become known as porter, named after the 'labouring classes' such as the porters who worked in the fish and fruit markets. Porter beer was a mixture of a heavy sweet ale and lighter bitter ales. In Dublin, St.James's Gate brewery was brewing porter by at least 1796. The Guinness brewery's emphasis on porter was such that, in 1799, it stopped brewing ale and concentrated solely on porter. For a while porter was known as 'entire', but in about 1900 Guinness developed a stronger porter which became known as stout (as in 'a stouter porter'). The brewery's range included Double Stout, a stronger beer for the Irish market, and Single Stout mainly for the English market.

Arthur Guinness passed away in 1803. He was 73 years old. He had fathered 21 children, though only 10 had survived, and it was his eldest son, also named Arthur, who took over the reins of the family business. By 1833 Arthur Guinness Sons & Co had claimed the status of Dublin's largest brewery.

The company was always looking for new outlets and avenues and, in the early

1860s, it took to selling bottled beer. The bottles had the Guinness 'harp' logo printed on the labels. The 'harp' – which became world-famous – was registered as a trade mark on 18 August 1862 – this was one of the very early trade marks to be registered. The labels were printed at the brewery.

Whereas the brewery's production destined for local customers was usually dispatched by horse and cart, a substantial proportion of the output was destined for farther afield. Much of this 'export' traffic was loaded on to barges at the Grand Canal Harbour which was close to the brewery. The Grand Canal Harbour was adjacent to James's Street Harbour which had opened in 1779 as the original Dublin terminus of the Grand Canal, but the real boon to Guinness's came in 1796 when a new canal link was opened to Ringsend Docks close to Dublin's main docks near the mouth of the River Liffey. The journey from James's Street Harbour via the new stretch of canal to Ringsend Docks was circuitous – it was about four miles – but it meant that Guinness traffic could be taken straight to the main docks to be transferred to larger seafaring vessels. In later years the brewery had another maritime outlet in the form of Victoria Quay on the River Liffey, though this, too, could handle only comparatively small vessels which had to transfer their cargoes to larger vessels at Dublin Docks. At one time Victoria Quay was connected to the original brewery by a horse-worked tramway. The general practice (in later years at least) was for Victoria Quay to be used for the dispatch of goods while the Grand Canal was used mainly by smaller barges bringing in barley from elsewhere in Ireland.

As we have seen, by 1833 the Guinness brewery was the largest in Dublin. The premises were enlarged and improved in 1865 and again in 1876, and by 1883 it was able to claim the status of the largest brewery in the world. It didn't stop there – there were further developments in 1899 and there was another major rebuilding programme in 1939, by which time the site covered some sixty acres and had 3,700 employees. Also, as some of our photographs show, there was further rebuilding work in the early 1950s.

Inevitably, the Guinness brewery generated work for other local businesses as well. The Guinness website (a really fascinating website – www.guinness.com – well worth a visit!) states that, in the 1930s, almost 14,000 people (excluding wives, families and other dependants) relied on the brewery for their income. In other words, one in every ten Dublin men looked to it for their livelihood, directly or indirectly. Another interesting snippet on the Guinness website explains that, as the wages paid to Guinness employees in those days were 10-20% above the local average and as there were the perks of guaranteed widows' pensions, paid holidays (almost unheard of in those days), free medical care, education and a host of other benefits, many Dublin mothers urged their daughters to find a Guinness employee as a husband. Another perk was that the workers received a free bottle of Guinness each day but, if they preferred not to drink, they could opt instead to receive additional cash in their pay packet. As the Guinness website puts it, the men were paid well to make a drink they were given to drink, and they were also paid well not to drink the drink they'd already been well paid to make. But we digress…

Narrow gauge

From a railway point of view, arguably the most interesting aspect of the Guinness brewery was its internal narrow gauge railway system. But why was a system of this nature required? As we have seen, the St.James's Gate brewery had its origins back in the 17th Century. It had initially grown in a fairly piecemeal manner and, to make maximum use of the available space, the buildings were close together. As the movement of materials around the site was for many years undertaken mainly by handcarts, and as outgoing road-borne goods were dispatched by horse and cart, the cramped nature of the site often caused congestion. Another factor which hampered transportation was that, as the brewery expanded, it was, in effect, on two working levels. When the company eventually considered laying an internal railway system, the confined nature of the site, plus the proliferation of restricted clearances of both width and height and the significant matter of the changes of levels completely ruled out using the broad gauge of 5ft 3in, and even the Irish narrow gauge of 3ft 6in was too big and unwieldy. Consequently, the internal system was laid to the very narrow gauge of 1ft 10in.

The narrow gauge system was constructed to the design of Samuel Geoghegan (pronounced 'Gaygan'), the company's chief engineer, and was installed mainly by the Dublin firm of Spence & Co. It was laid between 1873 and 1877 and ultimately comprised eight miles of track.

The railway was originally laid with 56lb iron tram rails fastened to longitudinal sleepers which in turn were laid on cross sleepers, but these were later replaced by 76lb steel rails with a web and flange, laid on conventional cross sleepers. However, the sleepering arrangements were often obscured as, throughout much of the brewery site and on Victoria Quay, they were covered by granite setts up to the level of the rails. The lines on Victoria Quay, incidentally, were extended at various times up to 1913, but were done away with in February 1963.

Narrow gauge traffic

The railway was used to move the raw materials (mainly malt and hops), spent grains, full and empty casks, coal for the many furnaces and the resultant ash and clinker. The fact that the extensions to the brewery had been built mainly on a hillside meant that there was a difference of some 60ft between the highest and the lowest level. The original and newer brewhouse, fermenting rooms, stables and malt and hop stores were on the upper level; the second or middle level had maltings and spent grain silos, while on the lower level were the cooperage shops and washing sheds, racking (filling of casks), warehouses and delivery platforms. Also on that level was Victoria Quay on the River Liffey.

By the mid-1890s the narrow gauge system was already handling an average of about 1,500 tons of traffic each working day. With the track layouts designed for easy movement, a locomotive with nine empty bogie wagons left the washing sheds, then went to the cask repairing shed where it left one empty wagon and hooked on in front a loaded wagon, then

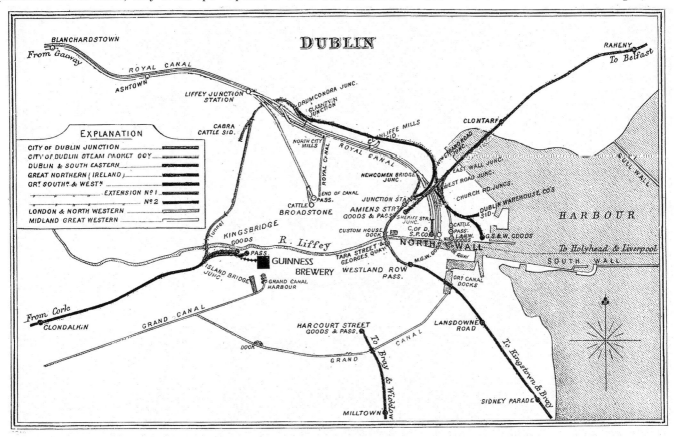

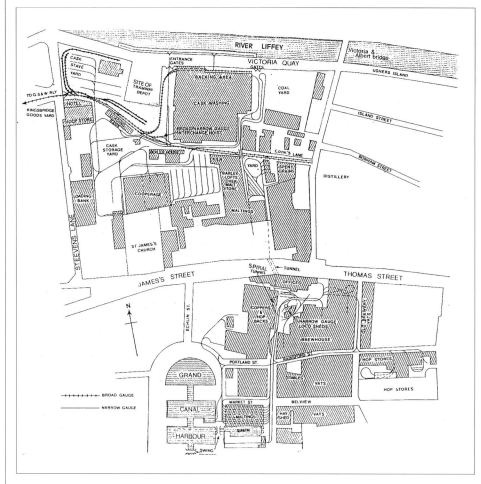

it was asked to perform, so it was soon relegated to hauling the lightweight visitors' passenger train.

Two more locomotives were delivered in 1876. These two were identical – built by Stephen Lewin & Co of Poole and designated No.2 HOPS and No.3 MALT, they were 0-4-0 well tanks with a single cylinder mounted on top of the boiler and had steel gearing to their solid steel wheels. They cost £366 each. Like their Sharp Stewart predecessor they, too, were rather underpowered. Another problem was that, although they were small and, therefore, comparatively lightweight, they caused considerable wear to the permanent way because they had no springs. Consequently, they finished up being used as stationary engines and were finally disposed of in 1914 and 1927 respectively.

Having found their first three locomotives to be unsuitable, Guinness turned to the more conventional and ordered two 0-4-0STs from Sharp Stewart. Delivered in 1878 at a cost of £597 each and designated Nos.4 and 5 in the Guinness fleet, these two had outside cylinders with Stephenson valve gear and weighed in at six tons each. These locomotives had one significant advantage in that their exhaust steam could be condensed in the tanks – this was of considerable benefit when working in the spiral tunnel However, in common with the original Sharp Stewart 0-4-0ST of 1875, they suffered from heavy wear caused by their motion picking up grime and dirt.

Still looking for a long-term solution to the motive power problem, Samuel Geoghegan drew up his own design for a locomotive which weighed less than $7\frac{1}{2}$ tons and could haul 18 tons on the spiral tunnel incline. To counteract the problem of the valve motion being close to the ground (and therefore vulnerable to dirt and dust), its two cylinders and motion were mounted on top of the boiler. The cylinders drove a horizontal crankshaft from which vertical connecting rods drove the rear wheels. A conventional coupling rod connected the rear wheels to the front ones (both sets of wheels being carried on leaf springs). It had 1ft 10in diameter wheels, $7\text{in} \times 8\frac{1}{2}\text{in}$ cylinders, a boiler pressure of 160lbs and weighed in at 7tons 8cwt. The order for its construction was placed with the Avonside Engine Company of Bristol; carrying Works No.1337, the locomotive was delivered in 1882. It cost £848.

Between 1887 and 1921 a further eighteen similar locomotives were built for the Guinness narrow gauge system, but none of these was built by Avonside. Instead, all were built by the local firm of William Spence of the Cork Street Foundry, Dublin. Although Spence's had experience in railway engineering – it was they who had installed the narrow gauge system at the Guinness brewery in the mid-1880s – the eighteen locomotives they built for Guinness's were the *only* locomotives they ever built. These remarkable little locomotives conformed to a loading gauge of just 5ft in width and

to the cooperage for new casks where it left one empty wagon and picked up a loaded one, and so on through the various yards and loading banks.

The speeds on the narrow gauge system were necessarily slow – often no more than walking pace and certainly never exceeding 10mph. This meant that, despite the complexity of the layout with its numerous triangular junctions and intersections, and although ten or more locomotives could be in use simultaneously, the system could be operated with only hand or flag signalling.

The spiral tunnel
As we have seen, the Guinness brewery was built on the side of a hill. Initially, a hydraulic wagon lift was provided to link the middle and upper sections of the site but, as the brewery became increasingly busy, the lift's capacity of just one wagon at a time became something of a hindrance. Samuel Geoghegan's ingenious solution to the problem was a spiral tunnel. A 25ft-deep, 125ft-diameter circular shaft was excavated vertically from the upper level, the shaft being lined with two concentric walls of brick. A single line of railway was laid inside the shaft – it descended from the upper level, curving on a radius of 61ft 3in and on a gradient of 1 in 40, and twisted through 2.65 turns to emerge at the middle level. The rail length within the spiral tunnel itself was 864ft, and there was another 400ft in the approach under James's Street. As can be seen on the accompanying map, a little beyond the lower exit of the tunnel the line crossed Cook's Lane by means of a bridge, then curved round, dropping at 1 in 42, to Victoria Quay.

The spiral tunnel, which cost £3,000 to construct, was an ingenious solution to a potentially difficult problem. As the tunnel had only a single track it required a reliable means of signalling – the only signalling anywhere on the brewery's narrow gauge system. A lever was positioned above the line at each end of the tunnel, the two levers being connected by a wire. Each lever had a weight at the top and, when entering the tunnel, the engine driver pulled a rope which was attached to the lever – this changed its position. To clear the line, the driver pulled a rope inside the tunnel as he passed – this pulled over the lever at the opposite end. The weights were too heavy for both levers to be pulled at once, so if the driver of an engine approaching from the other end found he could not move his lever, he knew that the tunnel was occupied. This basic system of line control remained in use until 1961 when it was replaced by electric colour light signals.

Narrow gauge locomotives
For the first two years of its existence the narrow gauge system was worked by horses. The first locomotive did not arrive until 1875. It was a diminutive Sharp Stewart 0-4-0ST which weighed just two tons and had a tank capacity of only 28 gallons. It cost £445. Not altogether surprisingly for such a small locomotive, its coupling rods came very close to the ground; this resulted in the motion becoming clogged by spilt grains and hops, grit and all manner of other dust and debris, and this inevitably meant that repairs were very regularly required. On top of that it was too light and underpowered for the demanding duties

A fine view of the Guinness site which, one imagines, was taken from one of the upper floors of Kingsbridge station building. The date is stated to be *circa* 1960. (We must admit that we originally had doubts about that date, mainly because of the Fiat 500 – we reckoned they didn't appear until the 1960s. But we are reliably informed that Fiat 500s made their debut as long ago as 1957. Case solved!) The entrance to the brewery is for the line from Kingsbridge goods yard. Just inside the brewery yard, CIE vans are being loaded with casks of draught Guinness. On the left of the picture are the new distribution sheds which were erected in the early 1950s partly on the site of the cask stave yard and partly on the site of the old tramway depot which Guinness had acquired in 1950. Between this new building and the loading bank roads is the hoist which was used for lifting the Spence narrow gauge locomotives on to the broad gauge haulage wagons. On the far right can be seen a mini-mountain of brand new casks. PHOTOGRAPH: AUTHOR'S COLLECTION

Guinness No.1 – the diminutive Sharp Stewart 0-4-0ST of 1875. It is seen with two of the three 'visitors carriages'; the date is 1895. For those of you watching in black and white, the locomotive is painted olive green. PHOTOGRAPH: AUTHOR'S COLLECTION

The second and third locomotives purchased for use at the Guinness brewery came from Stephen Lewin of Poole and were named MALT and HOPS. This picture was taken at Lewin's premises prior to their dispatch. Note the hinged chimney extension – lowered on MALT but upright on HOPS. This was an aid to draughting when lighting up. As is evident, the single cylinder was mounted on top of the boiler. The provision of a semi-circular footplate was to help the locomotives haul wagons around curves as tight as 12ft radius. The locomotives were designed so that they could double up as stationary engines; it seems that they spent most of the later years of their lives as such. PHOTOGRAPH: AUTHOR'S COLLECTION

6ft in height. The Spence locomotives were ingeniously designed so that they could be lowered on to a special broad gauge 'haulage wagon' which would enable them to be used, in effect, as broad gauge locomotives. When positioned on the haulage wagon, the locomotive's wheels engaged on rollers, the shafts of which had fixed gear wheels which engaged with the track axles of the haulage truck. The combined engine and haulage wagon had about double the hauling power of the engine alone. The 'haulage wagons' had a gear ratio of 3:1. They were also built by Spence – two were supplied in 1888, one in 1893 and one in 1903. They cost £450 each. *(We have not been able to determine whether the similar locomotive built by Avonside in 1882 was also capable of being mounted on a haulage wagon. We suspect not, but we would welcome enlightenment one way or the other, please – Ed.)*

The Spence locomotives had a Ramsbottom-type boiler with a circular firebox; they had steam brakes. They could haul 75 tons on the level and 18 tons on the gradient in the spiral tunnel. They had open footplates – this was commonplace for small industrial locomotives in the 1880s and 1890s, but whereas most industrial steeds which survived well into the 20th century eventually had some sort of cab fitted, the Spence locomotives never did.

Their principal dimensions were:
Cylinders: 7in x 8 1/2in
Wheel diameter: 1ft 10in
Wheelbase: 3ft 0in
Boiler diameter: 2ft 5in
Heating surface (tubes): 72.61 sq.ft.
Heating surface (firebox): 13.75 sq,ft.
Total heating surfaces: 86.36 sq.ft.
Grate area: 3.24 sq.ft.
Boiler pressure: 180 lbs
Weight: 7 tons 8 cwt
Water capacity: 80 gallons
Coal capacity: 3 1/2 cwt
Tractive effort: 2,900 lbs

The narrow gauge locomotives were accommodated in a part-roundhouse type of engine shed which was situated above the spiral tunnel. The turntable giving access to the shed roads was the only 'table on the brewery railway system. Should any reversals be required, locomotives could use one of the numerous triangles on the system.

As the years progressed it became increasingly apparent that the diminutive Spence locomotives could not go on indefinitely. Consequently, in the late 1940s Guinness looked across the water to the well-known maker of industrial diesel locomotives, F.C.Hibberd & Co Ltd of Park Royal in North London. Hibberd had already supplied two diesel locomotives to the Guinness brewery which had been built almost next door in

Park Royal in the mid-1930s, so it seems that a good working relationship had already been established.

Between 1947 and 1950 Hibberd supplied twelve 37hp narrow gauge diesels to the Dublin brewery. The last (Guinness No.36) did not actually arrive in Dublin until the autumn of 1951 as it was displayed at the Festival of Britain Exhibition on the South Bank in London prior to delivery.

The diesels were painted in the company's standard livery of dark blue. They were kept fully-employed – in the course of an ordinary working day, a locomotive, crewed by a driver and conductor, could move up to 8,000 casks on 27 bogie flats. That was a considerable feat for a small locomotive on such a complex layout. The arrival of the diesels enabled ten of the Spence locomotives and their Avonside predecessor to be taken out of service and scrapped. Nevertheless, steam and diesel worked alongside each other for several years. The last ordinary steam working on the narrow gauge was in 1957, after which the diesels prevailed.

Transfer hoist
As mentioned above, the Spence locomotives were designed so that they could be lifted on to 'haulage wagons' for use on the broad gauge. To lift the locomotives a special hoist was installed

in the Central Railway Receiving Yard. It was constructed of two 'A'-frames with a connecting bridge with beams at the top. On the bridge was situated the lifting gear, connected to a heavy inverted 'U' bar which straddled the narrow gauge locomotive. The lift was initially hydraulically powered but was later converted for electric operation.

Broad gauge

The Guinness brewery gained a rail connection to the outside world in 1875 when a single line almost 700 yards in length was laid betwen the Great Southern & Western Railway's Kingsbridge Goods Yard and the brewery. The line was laid to the Irish broad gauge of 5ft 3in, and for about 500 yards of its length was set into the roadway in 'street tramway' fashion.

During the First World War, incidentally, a siding was laid from the Guinness tramway into a Munitions Inspection Bond. This siding was worked by Guinness at no charge, but was removed after hostilities ended.

At the end of the 'street tramway' section the line crossed Steevens Lane to enter the brewery site. Inside the site the line reached what was known as the Central Railway Receiving Yard where it divided into several sidings, some of which served loading banks which were protected by canopies. In the 1920s a two-road engine shed was built here for Guinness' own locomotives.

On the north side of the Receiving Yard a siding diverged towards Victoria Quay – here casks could be loaded into (and empties unloaded from) Guinness's own steam barges. Back at the Receiving Yard, the longest siding continued in an easterly direction through the middle of the brewery site, serving several large cask storage areas, the large maltings and the spent grain silos, and terminated at the east end of Cook's Lane. Including all the sidings, the broad gauge system comprised about two miles of trackwork.

The broad gauge lines were laid with 80lb steel grooved and flanged rails. The groove was above the web, so engines and wagons ran on their wheel flanges. Evidently a similar grooved rail was in use by the GSWR for their 'Point Store' at North Wall at Dublin Docks.

Broad gauge traffic

Traffic on the broad gauge lines was initially hauled by horses. On the 'street tramway' section between the brewery and Kingsbridge Goods Yard this was more or less obligatory as the Act of Parliament which authorised the line prohibited '...the use of steam or atmospheric locomotion, or the use of ropes connected to a stationary steam engine'. Apart from horse-power or possibly man-power, there weren't too many alternatives.

Even before the brewery had been directly connected to the goods yard, Guinness's had seen the advantages of rail transport. The Guinness family were pro-railway (by the mid-1860s they had already invested a whopping £86,000 in Irish railway stock) and in 1867 Sir Benjamin Lee Guinness had made an agreement with the MGWR to transport porter to Galway, one of several similar arrangements. By 1872 Guinness's total trade with the railways had been worth £1,000,000.

Returning to the matter of the 'street tramway' section of line, locomotive working was finally authorised in 1901 but, in keeping with then current legislation, there were numerous restrictions. Trains had to be preceded by a man with a red flag, operations could take place only between 8.00am and 8.00pm, the speed could not exceed that at which a man could walk, locomotives had to have their motion and wheels covered, the locomotive had to have a warning bell which had to be rung, and a train could comprise no more than thirty wagons.

The rail connection at Kingsbridge Goods Yard gave Guinness direct access to the GNR(I) and the MGWR systems, thus eliminating time consuming and costly double handling. At the goods yard Guinness initially had three sidings specifically allotted to them, and a fourth was added sometime in the 1880s. From *circa* 1914 seven sidings were allotted to the Guinness traffic; this was still the case until the cessation of rail traffic in 1965.

Broad gauge locomotives

As we have seen, the narrow gauge Spence locomotives could be mounted in 'haulage wagons' for use on the broad gauge. This form of motive power was considered satisfactory for broad gauge operations for several years, and from 1901 the haulage wagons were also used on the 'street tramway' section between the brewery and Kinsgbridge Goods Yard. They were permitted a maximum loading of 13 wagons on this section.

The brewery did not acquire its first purpose-built broad gauge locomotive until 1912. This machine was built by Straker & Squire of London, a company better known as builders of omnibuses,

A *circa* 1911 view of the scald bank at the cask washing shed – this is where empty casks were inspected, cleansed and passed fit for racking. One of the 'demounted' Spence locomotives poses on the narrow gauge while the broad gauge wagons on the left are being handled by horses. PHOTOGRAPH: AUTHOR'S COLLECTION

A rake of four-wheeled tippers loaded with malt for the brewhouse are hauled by one of the Spence locomotives (out of view). As an aid to getting one's bearings, the train is approaching the brewhouse from the south – Rainsford Street is off to the right and Portland Street to the left. This picture seems to have been taken in the early 1960s. PHOTOGRAPH: AUTHOR'S COLLECTION

and had a 4-cylinder petrol engine which was rated at 90bhp at 500rpm. It was 15ft long, 8ft wide, and had air brakes and a rotary hand brake. It had a fairly complex method of transmission, and this seems to be one of the reasons why it had a fairly short operational life. It was withdrawn from service in 1916 and scrapped in 1921. Unfortunately, no photographs of this machine seem to exist, but an article in the journal of the Irish Railway Record Society states that it 'bore a remarkably close resemblance to a haulage truck'. Sounds intriguing!

Presumably in anticipation of the Straker & Squire machine being taken out of service, in 1914 Guinness purchased a conventional 0-4-0ST from Hudswell Clarke of Leeds. As W/No.1079, it had 15in x 22in outside cylinders, 3ft 4in wheels and weighed 24 tons. It had a brass bell on the right-hand side of the footplate – a requirement for working the 'street tramway' between the brewery and Kingsbridge Goods Yard. A similar locomotive was purchased from Hudswell Clarke in 1919. This was W/No.1152.

It appears that, as well as shunting inside the brewery complex, the Hudswell Clarkes took over most of the transfer trips to and from Kingsbridge Goods Yard. There seems to be little evidence of the Spence 'haulage wagons' being used on the 'street tramway' after the acquisition of the Hudswells.

In 1949 Guinness purchased a brand new broad gauge 0-4-0 diesel-mechanical shunter from Hudswell Clarke. Carrying W/No.D700, it had an eight-cylinder Davey Paxman engine, weighed in at 32 tons and was fitted with 'skirts' for use on the street tramway. It was designated No.4 in the broad gauge fleet and was named GUINNESS, the name being sported on a brass plate.

Rolling stock – narrow gauge

Due to the specialised nature of the products to be transported, there was not too much variety in the narrow gauge wagon fleet. The most numerous were four-wheeled side tippers; designed by Samuel Geoghegan, they were unsprung, had a tare weight of 15cwt, and their 3ft wheelbase was designed to negotiate curves of just 12ft radius. The bodies, which had a capacity of 80 cubic feet, were built of $^1/_8$in steel plate; they could be either completely or partially tipped. Many of these wagons were fitted with tarpaulin or hinged metal covers and were used for perishable malt. Other open wagons were used for coal, the removal of furnace ash and clinker, and spent grains and hops.

There were also several eight-wheeled bogie flats which were used to transport wooden casks and to carry lengthy pokes (sacks) of hops. Built of timber, they weighed just 28cwt. Their coupling bars

and dumb buffers were at the same height as the tippler wagons; the coupling bars were fixed to the bogies and not to the platform, thereby allowing easier passage over the sharp curves. The bogie flats could carry up to 31 empty casks of barrel size, stacked in three layers, or about half that number of full casks.

It is known that, in 1888, the Guinness wagon fleet comprised 177 vehicles. When the railway system was at its peak there were about 400 side tippers, 120 bogie flats, a few specialised wagons for engineering purposes and a small number of tank wagons.

There were also four 4-wheeled open 'toast rack' passenger coaches. Each could carry up to ten passengers on wooden slatted seats (albeit with cushions) and was covered by a striped canvas awning. These coaches were introduced in the 1880s and were used for taking parties of visitors around the site; looking rather smart with their dark blue paintwork, they remained in service until as late as 1964.

Rolling stock – broad gauge

Despite making extensive use of the Irish railway system for the movement of its goods, Guinness never owned any broad gauge wagons. Guinness relied instead on railway company-owned wagons, and all three of the major Irish railway companies – the GS&WR, GNR(I) and the M&GWR

Two of the famous Spence locomotives, Nos.22 and 24, pause between duties some time in the early 1960s. No.22 has its haulage chain hooked up, but there is no sign of any chain on No.24. PHOTOGRAPH: AUTHOR'S COLLECTION

– kept a number of covered vans exclusively for the Guinness trade, some of which had the company name painted on them.

Consequently, a variety of broad gauge wagons were to be seen at the brewery yard. In the early days of the 1880s some open-topped cattle wagons were used for moving casks. Open wagons were used for bringing in coal and for taking out ash, and also to take away the spent grains which were distributed to farmers around

A superb period view of a narrow gauge malt wagon train at the brewery. Underneath this area was the spiral tunnel. On the right is the part-roundhouse narrow gauge engine shed – a sort of St.Blazey, but a tad smaller and without the Prairies. PHOTOGRAPH: AUTHOR'S COLLECTION

ARTHUR GUINNESS SON & Co Ltd – summary of locomotives

Makers abbreviated thus:
AE – Avonside Engine Co; **FH** – F.Hibberd; **HC** – Hudswell Clarke; **SL** – Stephen Lewin; **SS** – Sharp Stewart; **STS** – Straker-Squire; **WS** – William Spence

(a) 1ft 10in gauge (all acquired new)

No.	Type	Maker; works no.	Wheels	Cylinders or h.p.	Built	Disposal
1	0-4-0ST	SS; 2477		(o)	1875	Scrapped 1913
2 *	0-4-0WT	SL -		6¼" x 8" (o)	1876	Scrapped 1914
3 *	0-4-0WT	SL -		6¼" x 8" (o)	1876	Scrapped 1927
4	0-4-0T	SS; 2764	1' 6"	6½" x 8" (o)	1878	Scrapped 1925
5	0-4-0T	SS; 2785	1' 6"	6½" x 8" (o)	1878	Scrapped 1925
6	0-4-0T	AE; 1337	1' 10"	7" x 8½" (o)	1882	Scrapped 1947
7	0-4-0T	WS -	1' 10"	7" x 8½" (o)	1887	Scrapped 11.1948
8	0-4-0T	WS -	1' 10"	7" x 8½" (o)	1887	Scrapped 11.1948
9	0-4-0T	WS -	1' 10"	7" x 8½" (o)	1887	Scrapped 11.1949
10	0-4-0T	WS -	1' 10"	7" x 8½" (o)	1891	Scrapped 11.1949
11	0-4-0T	WS -	1' 10"	7" x 8½" (o)	1891	Scrapped 11.1949
12	0-4-0T	WS -	1' 10"	7" x 8½" (o)	1891	Scrapped 8.1954
13	0-4-0T	WS -	1' 10"	7" x 8½" (o)	1895	(P) To Narrow Gauge Museum Trust, Towyn, 1956
14	0-4-0T	WS -	1' 10"	7" x 8½" (o)	1895	Scrapped 8.1951
15 ‡	0-4-0T	WS -	1' 10"	7" x 8½" (o)	1895	(P) To Colonel Kidd, Maidenhead, Co Laois, c.1965
16	0-4-0T	WS -	1' 10"	7" x 8½" (o)	1902	Scrapped 8.1951
17	0-4-0T	WS -	1' 10"	7" x 8½" (o)	1902	(P) To Guinness Museum, Dublin, c.1966
18	0-4-0T	WS -	1' 10"	7" x 8½" (o)	1902	Scrapped 8.1951
19	0-4-0T	WS -	1' 10"	7" x 8½" (o)	1902	Scrapped 8.1951
20	0-4-0T	WS -	1' 10"	7" x 8½ (o)	1905	(P) To Belfast Transport Museum 4.1956
21	0-4-0T	WS -	1' 10"	7" x 8½" (o)	1905	Sold (details unknown) c.1975
22 ‡	0-4-0T	WS -	1' 10"	7" x 8½" (o)	1912	‡ Frame to Winn Technology, Co Cork, 1973
23	0-4-0T	WS -	1' 10"	7" x 8½" (o)	1921	(P) To Brockham Museum, Surrey, 9.1966
24	0-4-0T	WS -	1' 10"	7" x 8½" (o)	1921	Scrapped 1967
25	4w DM	FH; 3068		3-cyl 37hp	1947	Still on site or (P) – see note below
26	4w DM	FH; 3255		3-cyl 37hp	1948	Still on site or (P) – see note below
27	4w DM	FH; 3256		3-cyl 37hp	1948	To Hendron Bros, Drumcondra, c.1973
28	4w DM	FH; 3257		3-cyl 37hp	1948	To Hendron Bros, Drumcondra, c.1973
29	4w DM	FH; 3258		3-cyl 37hp	1948	To Hendron Bros, Drumcondra, c.1973
30	4w DM	FH; 3259		3-cyl 37hp	1948	To Hendron Bros, Drumcondra, c.1973
31	4w DM	FH; 3446		3-cyl 37hp	1950	(P) To Irish Narrow Gauge Trust, Dromod, 2.2001
32	4w DM	FH; 3444		3-cyl 37hp	1950	Still on site
33	4w DM	FH; 3445		3-cyl 37hp	1950	To Hendron Bros, Drumcondra, c.1973
34	4w DM	FH; 3448		3-cyl 37hp	1950	To Hendron Bros, Drumcondra, c.1973
35	4w DM	FH; 3449		3-cyl 37hp	1950	(P) To Ulster Folk & Transport Museum, Cultra, 1977
36	4w DM	FH; 3447		3-cyl 37hp	1950 ¶	Still on site

* No.2 named HOPS; No.3 named MALT
‡ Boiler of No.15 fitted to frames of No.22 in 1956 – the 'rebuild' then ran as No.15
¶ Exhibited at Festival of Britain Exhibition in London and not delivered to Dublin until 1951
(P) Locos preserved:
   No.13 now at the Narrow Gauge Museum, Tywyn
   No.15 now at Stradbally Steam Museum, Co Laois
   No.17 now at the Guinness Museum, Dublin
   No.20 now at the Ulster Folk & Transport Museum, Holywood
   No.23 now at Amberley Chalk Pits Museum, West Sussex
   No.25 or No.26 – one of these two is at the Irish Narrow Gauge Trust at Dromod, presumably as a source of spares. The other is still at the brewery. Neither
has any means of identification so it is impossible to determine which is which
   No.31 now at the Irish Narrow Gauge Trust, Dromod
   No.35 now at the Ulster Folk & Transport Museum, Holywood

(b) 5ft 3in gauge (all acquired new)

No.	Type	Maker; works no.	Wheels	Cylinders or h.p.	Built	Disposal
1	4w PM	STS; -	2' 11"	90hp	1912	Scrapped 1921
2	0-4-0ST	HC; 1079	3' 4"	15" x 22" (o)	1914	Scrapped 7.1965
3	0-4-0ST	HC; 1152	3' 4"	15" x 22" (o)	1919	(P) To Railway Preservation Society of Ireland, 6.1965
4 *	0-4-0DM	HC; D700	3' 0"	8-cyl 204hp	1949	Scrapped 6.1966

* No.4 named GUINNESS
(P) Loco preserved:
   No.3 now at the Downpatrick Railway Museum, Downpatrick

Ireland for use as animal feed. For the M&GWR's part, it had two 8-ton and 23 10-ton wagons, built in 1898 and in 1916, all of which had the Guinness lettering in white. The GNR(I) had two types of 20-ton bogie wagons – they had the Guinness lettering painted across the two central doors on each side. The first design of *circa* 1896 had diamond framed bogies with double-spoked wheels, while the later design had pressed steel Fox's bogies. The capacity of the bogie wagons was equivalent to two four-wheeled vans, but the bogie wagons were not popular with the men as the narrow double doors hindered rapid loading and unloading.

With the formation of CIE – the Transport Company of Ireland – in 1945 several of the GNR(I) bogies were taken into stock, but the Guinness wording was

soon removed. The CIE adapted some GNR(I) Conflats for the new Guinness bulk tanks in the late 1950s. This adaptation required pieces of timber shaped to fit the circular tanks to be fixed to the floors. The first vehicles to be adapted were four-wheeled flat wagons which carried three out-of-line 504-gallon tanks; later modifications enabled the three tanks to be fixed in line.

Later years

Guinness gradually switched to containerised transportation. At the Kingsbridge transfer yard (which was renamed Heuston in 1966), a Liebherr gantry crane was installed in 1968 to offload Guinness's demountable containers on to bogie flats, two units to a wagon. The same crane was also used for

lifting containerised small draught beer kegs from open wagons on to Guinness's own semi-trailer road vehicles which ran a shuttle service between the brewery and the transfer yard. Each container contained carried 90 kegs, six wide and loaded to a single depth. Two could be loaded on to a bogie flat.

The movement of containers between the brewery and Kinsgbridge Goods Yard sometimes caused problems on the street tramway so Guinness abandoned the tramway and used road transport between the brewery and the yard. The tramway closed on 15 May 1965 and the three Guinness broad gauge locomotives were taken to the yard for storage while awaiting a decision as to their futures. One of the Hudswell Clarke 0-4-0STs was saved by the Railway Preservation

Society of Ireland, but the other two locomotives were scrapped.

With the cessation of inward and outward goods by rail, it was inevitable that the usage of the internal narrow gauge system at the brewery declined. However, it did not close altogether until 5 August 1975. Although the internal narrow gauge system had been 'all diesel' since 1957, at the time of closure in 1975 one of the Spence steam locomotives was still on site. That said, it had been out of use for some time. Happily, five of the Spence locomotives and one of the haulage wagons were saved for preservation. Three of the Hibberd diesels escaped cutting up but, although two are preserved, it seems that the third (either No.24 or 25 – the identity is not known) exists only as a source of spares for one of the others. Details are given in the accompanying table.

The run-down of narrow gauge operations was such that, by 1975, six of the Hibberd diesels had already been sold to Hendron Bros, a firm of dealers at Drumcondra; this left six other diesels on site. When members of the Industrial Railway Society visited the brewery in 1983 they were surprised to find five of the diesels still there, albeit dumped out of use. Even more surprising, perhaps, is that, at the time of writing (August 2002) three are still there.

Today, high capacity container tanks are sent to Belgium, which is Guinness's largest Continental customer. Daily liner

Above. **The structure on the right is the hoist which was used for lifting the Spence narrow gauge locomotives on to their broad gauge haulage wagons. One of the empty wagons can be seen almost underneath the hoist. On the left is one of the Spence locomotives mounted on a haulage wagon – its train is formed of the open cattle wagons which were used to carry casks in the early days. PHOTOGRAPH: AUTHOR'S COLLECTION**

Below. **A good view of two of the Spence locomotives. Note the spiked track. PHOTOGRAPH: AUTHOR'S COLLECTION**

trains between Dublin and Belfast run on Mondays to Fridays and include between three and five of the 20ft ISO container tanks of draught stout. Stout is also despatched by rail to Waterford, Cork, Galway, Limerick, Sligo and Ballinasloe, while inwards traffic includes containerised barley and malt chiefly from south of Dublin. All in all, Guinness is still a major customer of CIE, contributing revenue in excess of £1,000,000 p.a.

..........ooooo00Oooooo..........

As we have seen, the Guinness brewery railway system included an impressive number of unique features – the Spence locomotives, the haulage wagons, the spiral tunnel, to name just a few. So we'll close by pointing out that the Guinness company itself is famous for another unique feature – in contrast to all the other major British and Irish breweries, Guinness is alone in not owning one single pub.

Author's note: I would like to acknowledge the assistance with information and the use of many photographs from Arthur Guinness Son & Co. Information has also been gleaned from the Irish Railway Record Society, especially the article in their journal of October 1966 by R.C.Flewitt. Reference has been made to John E. King's article Containers Prominent in CIE's Guinness Traffic. *The*

classic reference, although limited, is Samuel Geoghegan's own article in the July 1888 edition of The Engineer. *I would also like to acknowledge with gratitude the help given me by the late Jim Peden of the Industrial Railway Society; thanks also to Paul Hood for information about Guinness's ships and to Russell Wear of the Industrial Locomotive Society.*

Above. Looking through the entrance gateway to the brewery on 29 October 1951. One of the haulage wagons propels a CIE van towards the loading bank. The steelwork in the distance is for the new distribution sheds which were seen in their completed form in one of our earlier pictures. PHOTOGRAPH: DESMOND COAKHAM

Sporting the standard livery of Royal Blue, Hibberd 'Planet' diesel No.34 poses at Victoria Quay with a rake of bogie wagons. Each of the barrels contains 36 gallons of Guinness. Note the very sharp curve in the foreground. PHOTOGRAPH: AUTHOR'S COLLECTION

Killiney, one of the Guinness steam barges, chugs along the River Liffey some time in 1957. *Killiney* was one of nine barges built by the Liffey Dockyard, Dublin, between 1929 and 1931 specifically to convey Guinness between Victoria Quay and the Custom House Quay for transhipment to larger vessels. The barges were 80ft long and were 81 tons gross. All had been sold by 1961 following the closure of Victoria Quay. On the opposite side of the water is the Custom House itself. Stacked on the quayside are 504-gallon tanks of Guinness for loading on to *The Lady Gwendolen* which was built for

Arthur Guinness Son & Co at the Ardrossan Dockyard in Scotland and was launched in April 1953. She was registered in Liverpool. Her sister ship was *The Lady Grania*. Gwendolen's vital statistics were: 1,166 g.r.t, 213ft 2in in length, 36ft 1in beam, draught (summer) 12ft 7 $\frac{1}{4}$in, British Polar diesel engine, speed 11 knots, crew of 14 in single cabins. She was sold in 1976 to a Greek company and renamed *Paros* but was run down while at anchor in Ravenna Roads in November 1979.
PHOTOGRAPH: AUTHOR'S COLLECTION

Guinness everywhere! Full barrels are being rolled along the quayside and a lorry (the registration looks like ZJ8514) is unloading a tank of the stuff aboard the S.S.*Guinness*. Lying low down almost out of view on the right is one of Guinness's steam barges which has brought full casks down from Victoria Quay. As for the S.S.*Guinness*, she was built by the Ailsa Shipbuilding Company of Troon; she was launched in May 1931 and registered in London. Her dimensions were 1,151 g.r.t, 211ft 8in long, 34ft 4in beam, maximum draught 15ft 9 $\frac{1}{2}$in. She had a triple expansion engine and two Scotch boilers. Her first run was from Dublin to London but she was transferred to the Mersey trade in 1938. She was sold for scrap in 1963 and arrived at Faslane for breaking up on 12 June of that year.
PHOTOGRAPH: AUTHOR'S COLLECTION

Guinness No.2 – one of the Hudswell Clarke 0-4-0STs – trundles sedately along the highway (the maximum permissible speed was 10mph) with a train from the brewery to Kingsbridge goods yard. The year is probably 1964, the last full year of the street tramway's operation. Note the engine's large buffer heads – this was a feature of all the standard gauge engines and was to help prevent buffer locking on tight curves. PHOTOGRAPH: AUTHOR'S COLLECTION

Hudswell Clarke diesel No.4 approaches the brewery with a rake of wagons (including a cattle wagon for empty casks) from Kingsland goods yard on 27 March 1951. Note the 'skirt' covering the wheels – this was a legal requirement for working the 'street tramway' section. On the right is the departure side of Kingsbridge passenger station. PHOTOGRAPH: DESMOND COAKHAM

No.4 reverses away from the Guinness sidings at Kingsbridge goods yard on 27 March 1951. The nest of sidings visible in the yard were for the exclusive use of the Guinness traffic. On the extreme right of the picture are the passenger lines to Kingsbridge terminus. PHOTOGRAPH: DESMOND COAKHAM

Beskirted Hudswell Clarke No.2 takes water from the tank near the engine hoist (the top of the hoist can be seen on the right). The tank had been installed *circa* 1900 and could service two engines on adjacent roads. Two of the haulage wagons stand on the far roads. PHOTOGRAPH: AUTHOR'S COLLECTION

Top right. Broad gauge activity at the Guinness brewery, 1956. The building work on the right is for the new distribution sheds and has required the disconnection of one of the turnouts. PHOTOGRAPH: AUTHOR'S COLLECTION

Below. An untypically lacklustre Hudswell Clarke No.2 shunts CIE vans near the loading bank in 1965. PHOTOGRAPH: AUTHOR'S COLLECTION

Bottom right. For all you dieselophobics, doesn't this picture prove that an industrial diesel can look rather handsome? Hudswell Clarke No.4 *Guinness* shows off her smart number plate, nameplate and gleaming works plate while shunting at the cask loading platform, possibly not too long after she was delivered in 1949. The brass bell was another legal requirement for the engines which worked along the street tramway to and from Kingsbridge goods yard. PHOTOGRAPH: AUTHOR'S COLLECTION

This 20-ton bogie van was owned by the GNR(I) but, as the lettering indicates, was devoted exclusively to Guinness traffic. This vehicle had pressed steel Fox's bogies, while the earlier vehicles of 1896 had diamond framed bogies. PHOTOGRAPH: AUTHOR'S COLLECTION

From the late 1950s CIE started adapting some wagons to take 504-gallon Guinness tanks. Some of these wagons – with the timber adaptors – are lined up on the left at Kingsbridge goods yard. The lorry in the foreground is a Bedford TK. If your editor's memory of his HGV days is accurate, a TK's reverse gear was perilously close to first. A teensy-weensy little misjudgement, and it could scare the hell out of the driver behind when you were pulling away – or *thinking* you were pulling away – in a queue of traffic. PHOTOGRAPH: AUTHOR'S COLLECTION

Preservation days – take one. Guinness No.15 was saved by Guinness and put on display at the company's museum. This picture shows it on the turntable outside the narrow gauge engine shed. PHOTOGRAPH: AUTHOR'S COLLECTION

The year is 1966 and the electric hoist carries out one of its last duties as it loads No.23 on to a broad gauge wagon for the first stage of its journey to the Brockham Museum in Surrey. When that museum closed in 1982 its exhibits were transferred to what became the Amberley Chalk Pits Museum in West Sussex. PHOTOGRAPH: AUTHOR'S COLLECTION

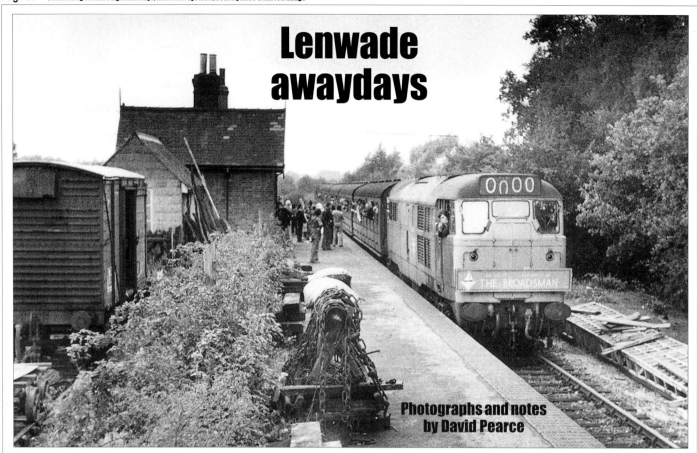

Lenwade awaydays

Photographs and notes by David Pearce

'Goods only' branch lines have always been a strong lure for enthusiasts' specials as they provide something a little bit different for those who wish to travel on lines which are usually out of bounds to passengers. In rural Norfolk, a number of lines had lost their passenger services in the 1950s and 60s but remained open – though often only in part – to goods traffic, so it was no surprise to find that surviving 'goods only' stubs of former main and branch lines were popular targets for specials.

One location which became a popular, if infrequent, target for specials and railtours was Lenwade on the former M&GN branch from Melton Constable to Norwich City. Lenwade had lost its ordinary passenger services in February 1959 but continued to handle trains from a concrete factory which had opened as recently as 1957 – the factory had its own private siding and frequently dispatched its goods by rail. Here is just a small selection of views of some of those railtours, now no longer possible since the goods traffic ceased in the 1980s and the rails were subsequently lifted. For some reason the trips to Lenwade always seemed to run in the early autumn – a mellow time was had by all!

Above. 2 October 1976: The Lea Valley Railway Club had the rather enterprising idea of running an excursion from London to deepest rural Norfolk using a set of Kings Cross suburban coaches. The mind boggles at the number of 'personal needs breaks' which were required en route, particularly beyond Norwich where toilet facilities were, and still are, very much at a premium! Nevertheless 'The Broadsman' comprised six coaches and was headed by a Class 31. (For the sake of other old dinosaurs like your editor, that's a Brush Type 2 – what used to be a D55XX in old money – Ed.). On arrival at Norwich the engine was taken off for refuelling and replaced by another Class 31, 31160, which continued to Lenwade via Wroxham, Aylsham (photo stop), and the Themelthorpe Curve. Once it had disgorged its passengers the train ran the few hundred yards beyond Lenwade to run round near the concrete factory before returning to pick up the passengers for the return leg. A further photo stop was put in at Reepham before arrival back at Norwich in the gathering gloom. At Norwich the train was reunited with the Class 31 which had brought it in from London in the morning; this engine, having refuelled, backed on and headed back to London. Our photograph shows the train arriving at the still clean but somewhat cluttered platform at Lenwade where a small gathering of locals had turned out.

17 September 1977: The Aylsham and District Rail Action Committee organised a special 'Silver Jubilee' train to commemorate (if that is the right word) the 25th anniversary of the withdrawal of passenger services on the Wroxham-County School branch on 15 September 1952. The train ran from Norwich to Lenwade and back and, because the Queen was also celebrating her Silver Jubilee, the train was suitably bedecked with flags and a headboard. That the headboard proclaimed 'Great Eastern' at this former M&GN outpost must have been a tad provocative to those who lamented the wholesale closure of the much-loved M&GN in 1959. The train was made up of a 3-car BRCW unit and a 2-car Cravens unit, obviating the need to run round once they had arrived at their destination. It seems as if all the world and his dog (well – one rough collie) were getting off the train to sample the heady delights of Lenwade and to photograph the occasion for posterity.

16 September 1978: The goods yard looks to be quite crowded with wagons on this occasion and, presumably, was a sight to gladden the hearts of the Railway Invigoration Society whose special had just arrived. Although the general goods facilities had been withdrawn from Lenwade back in October 1966, the sidings remained *in situ* and were often used for the storage of wagons in connection with the local concrete works. Once again a combination of locally-based Cravens and BRCW units had been provided for this excursion from Norwich. The train had called at Wroxham, Aylsham (for a visit to Blickling Hall) and Reepham for the local carnival. Looks as though it was a nice day for it!

29 September 1979: Hertfordshire Railtours organised an excursion from Bletchley which provided the novel experience of the train being hauled by a diesel shunter for the branch line leg of the tour. The train ran under reporting number 1Z85 and also provided passengers with the rare opportunity to grice the Wensum Curve at Norwich behind Class 47 No.47170. However, the honours of traversing the Lenwade stub fell to local Class 08 No.08250 which proceeded at what might be termed a stately (OK – pedestrian) pace, proudly sporting an 'Anglian Explorer' headboard. Again, as it was a loco-hauled train the engine had to run round beyond Lenwade. On this occasion the passengers were allowed to remain on board and cover the most southerly surviving tip of the former M&GN lines in Norfolk – exceedingly rare track indeed! This view looks southwards; 08250 has run round at the concrete works and is bringing the train back into the station.

NOT OUT OF THE ORDINARY – BRICKET WOOD STATION
Photographs by R.P.D.Sands, all taken in May 1955; captions by Bryan L.Wilson

Without wishing to do it down, Bricket Wood station on the Watford Junction-St.Albans Abbey branch is nothing special. It does not have a fascinatingly juicy history, it has never been an important junction or the terminus of an important line, it never had an engine shed, nor has it been the focus of some particularly intriguing train working. Its only claim to fame is that it hasn't got one. It is, to be blunt, a very ordinary station which has led a very ordinary existence. But within that very ordinariness lies Bricket Wood's appeal. There were – and still are – countless outer suburban stations throughout Britain, and Bricket Wood could be almost any one of them. These photographs show the almost forgotten mid-1950s face of such almost forgotten stations.

Bricket Wood station, 3¼ miles from Watford Junction on the LNWR's single-track branch from to St.Albans Abbey, opened with the line on 5 May 1858. The station's long-term future must have looked somewhat bleak when, just three months later, it was closed, the management having decided that there was insufficient traffic for both it and Park Street station, located 1½ miles nearer to St.Albans. But despite being closed to ordinary trains Bricket Wood station remained open to picnic parties, a request for the train to stop having to be made to the station master at St.Albans. Local pressure soon led to the station's permanent reopening, and it reappeared again in the public timetables for July 1861. The station originally comprised only a raised platform with a lean-to shed for shelter, but in 1903 the LNWR hierarchy approved the expenditure of £1,550 on improvements to the buildings and other items. This May 1955 view of the station front shows those improvements, perhaps best described as functional, albeit rather well maintained. Behind the station building on the right can be seen part of the Up platform awning; this awning had been extended at the same time as the station 'improvement' works.

BRICKET WOOD (Herts)
Miles 21.   Map Sq. 23.
Pop. 1,800.   Clos. day Tue.
From Euston.
3rd S'gle 3/4, Ret. 6/8, Day R. 5/10.
See table 54.

ABC Railway Guide,
March 1956.

By 1912 the point had been reached where the branch service needed to be increased beyond 15 trains each way per day, but this could not be done without provision of an intermediate passing loop. The construction of the loop and a new Down platform were approved on 16 October 1912 and the new facilities were brought into use in April 1913. This picture shows the passenger facilities which were provided on the new Down platform. The structure was a standard LNWR building of its time, raised on timbers in the manner of a glorified garden shed. The absence of a chimney suggests that the building had no heating. To the left of the building, an attractive gas lamp completes the scene.

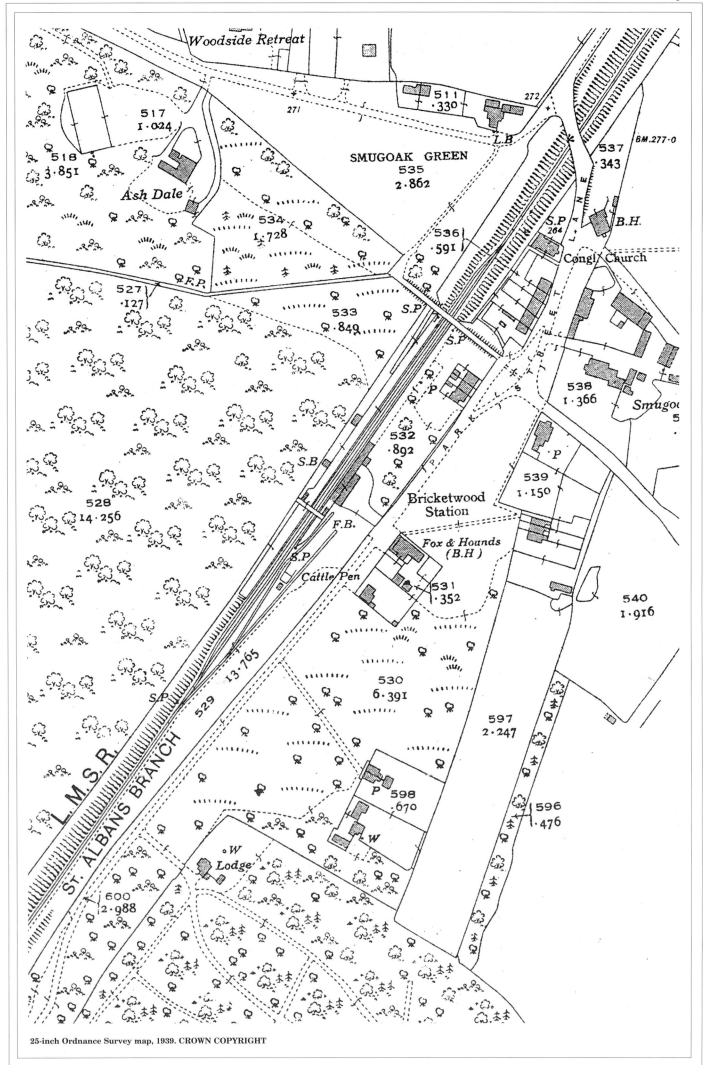

Woodside Retreat

517
1·024

518
3·851

Ash Dale

534
1·728

SMUGOAK GREEN
535
2·862

511
·330

272

L.B.

BM.277·0

537
·343

S.P.
264

B.H.

Congl Church

536
·591

527
·127

F.P.

533
·849

S.P.

S.P.

538
1·366

P

Smugoa

532
·892

S.B.

539
1·150

528
14·256

P

Bricketwood
Station

F.B.

S.P.

Cattle Pen

Fox & Hounds
(B.H)

531
·352

540
1·916

530
6·391

597
2·247

529   13·765

S.P.

L.M.S.R.

ST. ALBANS BRANCH

P   598
·670

596
·476

W

W

Lodge

600
2·988

We are looking in a south-westerly direction in the direction of Watford. The main station buildings with their large awning are on the Up platform on the left. The Way Out from the down platform via the bank to Smugoak Green is on the right. This scene is delightfully rural, but we are only 21 miles from Euston.

The Down platform, looking towards St.Albans. The LNWR 'Type 5' signal box was provided at the same time as the new loop in 1913. It boasted 18 levers of which 13 were in use in 1916. By that latter date Down trains could also use the Up platform (on which the main buildings were situated) provided, of course, that the crossing of an Up train was not required. At the time of the photograph (May 1955), the signal box was open from 5.50am until 11.55pm on Mondays to Fridays; it closed 10 minutes later on Saturdays because there was a later train, the 11.50pm from St.Albans which was timed to call at Bricket Wood at 11.57pm. On Sundays the box was open from 7.30am until 10.15pm. Although Bricket Wood station is still open today (more of which anon), the signal box closed on 7 August 1966 when Watford North-St.Albans became one single Electric Train Staff section.

Above. Looking out from the Down end of the station. The nearer of the two bridges carries a footpath over the railway while the bridge in the distance carries Park Street Lane across the line. The width of the second bridge betrays the fact that, in common with so many other branch lines, the Watford-St.Albans branch, although laid with only a single track, had been built wide enough for two lines of rails to allow for doubling at a future date. Also in common with so many other branch lines, doubling was never actually required. The signals are LNWR lower quadrants; the presence of the one on the right confirms that the Up platform could be used by Down trains.

Left. The signal box in close-up – and just look at the detail. It has large, 6ft-high windows with double handrails below the centre line (for cleaning the windows and to stop the signalman from falling out), and an overhanging roof with pinnacles atop. This type of box was standard for the remainder of the LNWR's existence; indeed, the design continued in use until 1930 when LMS designs took hold. The signalman is in the 'reclining' position; unless he is a candidate for the Guinness Book of Records (or was it the Book of Record Guinnesses?), one assumes that the legs at the top of the steps belong to a colleague. Above the box we have the once common telegraph pole and, down on ground level, the equally common signalman's bicycle. And what is that receptacle attached to the box to the left of the seat ? Possibly for used tickets from those using the Down side exit?

Back to the Down platform... The flower beds beyond the footbridge suggest that there were some enthusiastic gardeners among the station staff. To the right of the footbridge the station name has been spelt out in timber – another nice touch. The platform furniture also includes another nice gas lamp and a 'gallows' Way Out sign.

The long straight view towards Watford. The signal in the foreground is the Up starter, an LMS corrugated arm of the type introduced by that company on the Midland Division about 1925 and subsequently spread across their empire. The signals in the distance facing oncoming (Down) trains read for the Up and Down platforms. Not much is going on in the goods yard, it seems – the dock and the sidings are somewhat herbaceous – and this is ten years before the station was closed to freight.

Table 55

WATFORD AND ST. ALBANS (ABBEY)

THIRD CLASS ONLY

WEEKDAYS

Miles											SX	SO		SO	SO	SX	SO	SO	SX	SO	SO	SX	SX	
0	**Watford Junction** dep.	5 42	5 55	6 15	6 48	7 12	7 42	8 9	9 17	10 18	11 15	11 25	12 30	12 55	1 20	1 28	1 50	2 16	2 20	2 45	3 8	3 29	3 53	. . .
1⅛	Watford North	5 45	5 57	6 18	6 50	7 14	7 44	8 12	9 19	10 20	11 17	11 27	12 32	12 57	1 22	1 30	1 52	2 18	2 22	2 47	3 10	3 31	3 55	.
3⅜	Bricket Wood	. . .	6 3	6 26	6 57	7 21	7 51	8 19	9 25	10 26	11 23	11 33	12 38	1 4	1 29	1 36	1 58	2 26	2 28	2 53	3 16	3 37	4 2	. . .
4⅞	Park Street & Frogmore	.	6 7	6 30	7 1	7 25	7 55	8 23	9 29	10 30	11 27	11 37	12 42	1 8	1 33	1 40	2 2	2 30	2 32	2 57	3 20	3 41	4 6	.
6½	**St. Albans (Abbey)** arr.	. . .	6 12	6 35	7 7	7 30	8 0	8 28	9 34	10 35	11 32	11 42	12 47	1 13	1 37	1 45	2 7	2 35	2 37	3 2	3 25	3 46	4 11	. . .

WEEKDAYS—*continued*

	SO	SX	SX	SO	SX	SX	SO	SX	SX	SX	SO	SX	SX	SO	SX	SO	SX	SX	SO	SX	SO	SO		
Watford Junction dep.	4 0	4 25	4 53	5 0	5 25	5 48	6 0	6 13	6 35	6 58	7 0	7 23	7 48	8 0	8 29	9 0	9 10	9 55	10 0	10 38	10 45	11 30	. . .	. . .
Watford North	4 2	4 27	4 56	5 2	5 27	5 51	6 2	6 16	6 38	7 1	7 2	7 25	7 50	8 2	8 31	9 2	9 12	9 57	10 2	10 40	10 47	11 32	.	.
Bricket Wood	4 8	4 33	5 3	5 8	5 34	5 59	6 8	6 23	6 46	7 8	7 8	7 32	7 57	8 8	8 37	9 8	9 18	10 3	10 8	10 46	10 53	11 38	. . .	. . .
Park Street & Frogmore	4 12	4 37	5 7	5 12	5 38	6 3	6 12	6 27	6 50	7 12	7 12	7 36	8 1	8 12	8 41	9 12	9 22	10 7	10 12	10 50	10 57	11 42	.	.
St. Albans (Abbey) arr.	4 17	4 42	5 12	5 17	5 43	6 8	6 17	6 32	6 55	7 17	7 17	7 41	8 6	8 17	8 46	9 17	9 27	10 12	10 17	10 55	11 2	11 47	. . .	. . .

SUNDAYS

Watford Junction dep.	7 35	8 35	10 30	11 30	12 30	1 30	2 30	3 30	4 30	5 30	6 30	7 30	8 30	9 30	. . .	. . .	. . .	. . .	. . .	. . .
Watford North	7 37	8 37	10 32	11 32	12 32	1 32	2 32	3 32	4 32	5 32	6 32	7 32	8 32	9 32	.	.	.	.	.	.
Bricket Wood	7 43	8 43	10 38	11 38	12 38	1 38	2 38	3 38	4 38	5 38	6 38	7 38	8 38	9 38	. . .	. . .	. . .	. . .	. . .	. . .
Park Street & Frogmore	7 47	8 47	10 42	11 42	12 42	1 42	2 42	3 42	4 42	5 42	6 42	7 42	8 42	9 42	.	.	.	.	.	.
St. Albans (Abbey) arr.	7 52	8 52	10 47	11 47	12 47	1 47	2 47	3 47	4 47	5 47	6 47	7 47	8 47	9 47	. . .	. . .	. . .	. . .	. . .	. . .

WEEKDAYS

Miles												SX	SO	SX	SO	SO		SO		SO	SO	SX	
0	**St. Albans (Abbey)** dep.	. . .	6 15	6 45	7 13	7 42	8 8	8 37	8 53	9 38	10 45	11 37	12 8	12 50	12 55	1 20	1 50	2 16	2 45	3 8	3 29	3 55	. . .
1⅝	Park Street and Frogmore	.	6 18	6 48	7 16	7 45	8 11	8 40	8 56	9 41	10 48	11 40	12 11	12 53	12 58	1 23	1 53	2 19	2 48	3 11	3 32	3 58	.
3⅛	Bricket Wood	. . .	6 25	6 56	7 22	7 52	8 18	8 45	9 0	9 45	10 52	11 44	12 15	12 58	1 3	1 28	1 58	2 24	2 53	3 16	3 37	4 3	. . .
5⅜	Watford North	5 48	6 30	7 1	7 27	7 58	8 24	8 50	9 5	9 50	10 57	11 49	12 20	1 3	1 8	1 33	2 3	2 29	2 58	3 21	3 42	4 8	.
6½	**Watford Junction** arr.	5 51	6 35	7 5	7 31	8 2	8 28	8 54	9 10	9 54	11 1	11 53	12 24	1 7	1 12	1 37	2 7	2 33	3 2	3 25	3 46	4 12	. . .

WEEKDAYS—*continued*

		SX	SX	SO	SX	SX	SO	SX	SX	SX	SO	SX	SX	SO	SX	SO	SX	SX	SO	SX	SO	SO	
St. Albans (Abbey) dep.	4 25	4 55	5 24	5 24	5 50	6 12	6 25	6 38	6 58	7 22	7 25	7 48	8 9	8 25	8 49	9 25	9 30	10 15	10 25	11 0	11 5	11 50	. . .
Park Street and Frogmore	4 28	4 58	5 27	5 27	5 53	6 15	6 28	6 41	7 2	7 25	7 28	7 51	8 12	8 28	8 52	9 28	9 33	10 18	10 28	11 3	11 8	11 53	.
Bricket Wood	4 33	5 4	5 33	5 33	6 0	6 22	6 32	6 45	7 9	7 31	7 32	7 56	8 16	8 32	8 56	9 32	9 37	10 23	10 32	11 7	11 12	11 57	. . .
Watford North	4 38	5 9	5 39	5 38	6 5	6 27	6 37	6 50	7 14	7 36	7 37	8 1	8 21	8 37	9 1	9 37	9 42	10 28	10 37	11 12	11 17	12 2	.
Watford Junction arr.	4 42	5 13	5 43	5 42	6 9	6 32	6 41	6 55	7 18	7 40	7 41	8 5	8 25	8 41	9 5	9 41	9 46	10 32	10 41	11 16	11 21	12 6	. . .

SUNDAYS

St. Albans (Abbey) dep.	8 0	9 0	11 0	12 0	1 0	2 0	3 0	4 0	5 0	6 0	7 0	8 0	9 0	10 0	. . .	. . .	. . .	. . .	. . .	. . .
Park Street & Frogmore	8 3	9 3	11 3	12 3	1 3	2 3	3 3	4 3	5 3	6 3	7 3	8 3	9 3	10 3	.	.	.	.	.	.
Bricket Wood	8 8	9 8	11 8	12 8	1 8	2 8	3 8	4 8	5 8	6 8	7 8	8 8	9 8	10 8	. . .	. . .	. . .	. . .	. . .	. . .
Watford North	8 13	9 13	11 13	12 13	1 13	2 13	3 13	4 13	5 13	6 13	7 13	8 13	9 13	10 13	.	.	.	.	.	.
Watford Junction arr.	8 17	9 17	11 17	12 17	1 17	2 17	3 17	4 17	5 17	6 17	7 17	8 17	9 17	10 17	. . .	. . .	. . .	. . .	. . .	. . .

SO—Saturdays only. SX—Saturdays excepted.

LMR public timetable, 14 June to 19 September 1954.

Aha! A goods vehicle is hiding.... An LMS horse box awaits its quadruped occupant. So we end our survey on a high note – even if there is no life to be seen apart from the signalman and a mystery pair of legs, the horse box suggests that some sort of life is at least expected. Bricket Wood station is still open today, being served by about 30 trains each way on weekdays and 15 on Sundays between Watford Junction and St.Albans. The trains are Class 313 EMUs which are operated by Silverlink.

An Inspector Calls
by Don Townsley

WD Nos.15 and 14 venture up the test track at Hunslet's Jack Lane works on 1 May 1937 under the careful superintendence of the Government inspector. The leading locomotive has a straight-through exhaust pipe without a silencer whereas the second one has an exhaust gas conditioner for comparison purposes. These early 20hp Hudson Hunslets were fitted with the Ailsa Craig two-cylinder CF2 direct injection engine which was superseded from late 1939 by the indirect injection RF2 with Ricardo cylinder head. What cannot be seen is the hydraulic dynamometer between the coupling blocks of the two locomotives; this was used for recording the drawbar pull of the leading machine. PHOTOGRAPH: AUTHOR'S COLLECTION

It is May Day 1937 and although nobody is supposed to know – least of all Neville Chamberlain – preparations for war are proceeding apace. One aspect of the preparations is underway at Hunslet's Jack Lane works in Leeds where a pair of tiny 20hp Hudson Hunslet 2ft gauge locomotives are trundling up the test track. Our pictures show the locomotives under test. Driving the first is a suitably stern-faced and London-suited Government inspector, while a Hunslet fitter follows on behind in the second locomotive.

The 20hp Hudson Hunslet was introduced in 1937 as a standard locomotive for light railways throughout the world, and literally hundreds were built in the same basic form until 1950. Updated variations continued to appear until the mid-1980s. Intended at the outset to be built for stock, the first authorisation for this new design was given Hunslet order number 48000; this covered twelve locomotives which carried

works numbers 1830-1835 and 1860-1865. Of these, nine went to embryonic military establishments with six being delivered to the ammunition depot at Corsham, Wiltshire and three to the Royal Ordnance Factory which was being constructed by Sir Lindsay Parkinson & Co at Chorley, Lancashire.

The two seen here – No.14 and No.15 (HE 1860 and 1861) – were the last two of the initial Corsham six. The photographs were taken for a particular reason, namely to show the box which was fitted at the side of the engine on locomotive No.14. The box was a conditioner designed to remove the aldehydes from the exhaust and generally reduce the irritant fumes. It will be noted that No.15 is not thus fitted; neither were the previous four Corsham locomotives of this type.

At the time, exhaust conditioning was something new in diesel locomotives. The first serious attempt had taken place eight weeks earlier when a reduced-height

155/170hp standard gauge 0-6-0 had been delivered, also to Corsham, by Hunslet on 4 March 1937.

To understand why one of the Corsham 2ft gauge locomotives was fitted with exhaust conditioning equipment, we need to look briefly at Corsham itself. Back in the days of the GWR broad gauge, a connection (later converted to standard gauge) was laid on the up side at the east end of Box Tunnel to serve extensive underground stone mines. In 1936 the War Department extended the underground workings and initiated the development of a massive underground ammunition storage depot, hence the requirement for standard and narrow gauge locomotives. With associated and interconnected underground developments at Hawthorn, West Wells and Monkton Farleigh, the Corsham complex was eventually to find employment for five standard gauge and no less than 113 narrow gauge locomotives. The standard gauge was served by three Hunslet 0-6-0s and two

Fowler 0-4-0s, while the narrow gauge stud comprised 81 Hudson Hunslets and 32 Rustons.

As can be imagined, with such a huge stud of locomotives, a vast number of workers (7,500 men are reputed to have been involved at one time) and storage for 350,000 tons of ammunition, the emission of sparks and the generation of excessive temperatures had to be avoided. Corsham's standard gauge locomotives were fitted with full flameproof protective equipment and, after trials with 2ft gauge No.14, the other narrow gauge locomotives were retrospectively fitted with exhaust conditioners. Later machines had the conditioners fitted from new.

Such was the understandable need for secrecy at Corsham that extreme care was taken that personnel knew only their own little bit of activity and had no idea of the vastness of the place. The contemporary Hunslet records list the locomotives as being despatched to Corsham, Monkton Farleigh and Ridge Quarries, or to Sir Alfred McAlpine & Sons No.1 Depot at Corsham. (McAlpine's were the contractors for a large proportion of the new construction.) The majority of the depots in the Corsham area and the standard gauge railway there had closed by 1963 but the Ministry of Defence establishment at Corsham continued to make use of some of the narrow gauge system for a while longer. The Hudson-Hunslets had been dispensed with between 1943 and 1963, many having been repurchased by the Hunslet Engine Company and, after complete refurbishment, resold to customers all over the world. The type of motive power used for the residual narrow gauge operations after 1963 is unknown.

HUDSON HUNSLET 20hp LOCOMOTIVES		
Engine: Ailsa Craig CF2		
Power and Speed: 20 bhp @ 1200rpm		
Loco weight: 3 tons 6 cwts		
Speeds: 3.5 and 7 mph (both in forward gear or reverse)		
Ratio of adhesion: 4.06 to 1		
Rail gauge: 60 cms and upwards		
Minimum rail weight: 12/14 lbs per yard		
Minimum curve radius: 30 ft.		
Overall width: 3ft 6in (for 60cms and 2ft gauge)		
Fuel tank capacity: 5 gallons		
Loads hauled (excluding weight of locomotive):		
Gear:	1st	2nd
Speed:	0-3.5mph	3.5-7mph
Tractive effort:	1,820lbs	910lbs
On the level:	88 tons	42.5 tons
1 in 100:	40 tons	18.5 tons
1 in 50:	25 tons	11 tons

The exhaust gas conditioner on No.14 contained baffles to 'scrub' the exhaust before its emission to the atmosphere. Not a perfect solution but one which was well fitted to the urgency of the situation and labour aspirations of the time. The hand klaxon will be noted; the electric lighting was an optional extra. The four-position slotted coupler was cast integrally with the frame and, with its long pin to engage a single link, survived for a number of years but ultimately gave way on future new locomotives to a separate buffer block with rubber mounting strips. Hand starting, with a kick like a mule, was the norm; electric starting was an optional extra but it was frowned upon because of the extreme hazards imposed by batteries and sparks. The light was directly supplied by a 'protected' dynamo and cable. PHOTOGRAPH: AUTHOR'S COLLECTION

THE REAL EAST LONDON

A journey from North Woolwich to Stratford (Low Level)
Photographs by John R. Bonser; commentary by Bryan L. Wilson

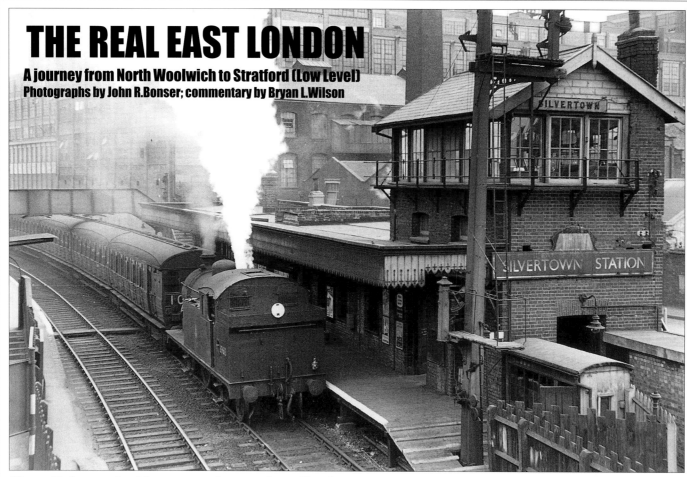

Above. Before embarking on our journey from North Woolwich, here's a taster of what the North Woolwich line was all about – a Stratford N7 0-6-2 tank and a Quint-Art set calls at Silvertown with the 12.46pm (SO) North Woolwich to Palace Gates on 16 March 1957. Improvisation is apparent with the headcode, an ordinary lamp having replaced a black centred disc at the bottom right of the bunker. "Someone pinched it. Honest, guv". Access to the station is beneath the signal box through that black hole leading into the dim gas-lit booking hall. The box is elevated to give the signalman a clear view of the Silvertown Tramway which ran behind the station buildings. Note the lower repeater signal arms; these were provided because the station canopy blocked the view of main arms for drivers of Up trains when they were standing in the station. That interesting hut below the signal looks like an old vehicle of some sort, but what does its 'serving hatch' dispense? The name Silvertown came from one Mr.S.W.Silver who brought his waterproof clothing works here in 1852. The area gradually developed, and Silvertown station was opened in June 1863. Eventually, Silvertown became a place where chemicals, creosote and manure industries stood cheek by jowl with jam, soap and sugar factories. This scene just oozes 1950s East London.

Left. Our trip commences at North Woolwich. The railway arrived there in 1847, reaching a place '...with poor uninhabited houses and a tavern'. As if to reflect their less than salubrious surroundings, the original station buildings were made of timber, but in 1854 they were replaced by this Italianate style frontage. This picture was taken on 13 June 1969. Ten years later a new entrance, much less imposing, was provided on the south side and in September 1984 the original building – with its status as a Grade 2 Listed Historical Building – became the North Woolwich Old Station Museum, housing a variety of Great Easternry.

Above. In the early days of the railways there was no crossing of the Thames east of Tower Bridge, so it fell to the railway companies to provide access from one side to the other. At Woolwich, access was provided by a passenger ferry between a pier near North Woolwich station and another pier off High Street, Woolwich, on the south bank of the river. The Woolwich ferry became an essential part of life for those workers (workers were some years ahead of commuters) who needed to get to the 'proper' Woolwich on the other side. The 'proper' Woolwich, incidentally, was referred to by the Great Eastern as 'South Woolwich', a title which had no official standing whatsoever! But there again, it was the GE which had also coined the name North Woolwich for the 'poor uninhabited houses and a tavern' on the north bank – before the GER's arrival that community had not had a 'proper' name of its own. As for the railway ferry, it started operating soon after the North Woolwich branch opened in 1854 and continued until the end of September 1908. The London County Council had started a Free Ferry at the same place in March 1889 – there was no 'unfair competition' legislation in those days – whereas the GE crossing had cost one penny. This picture, which was taken on 13 June 1969, shows the passenger walkway from North Woolwich station to the landing stage. A tug is making use of the landing stage for a mooring.

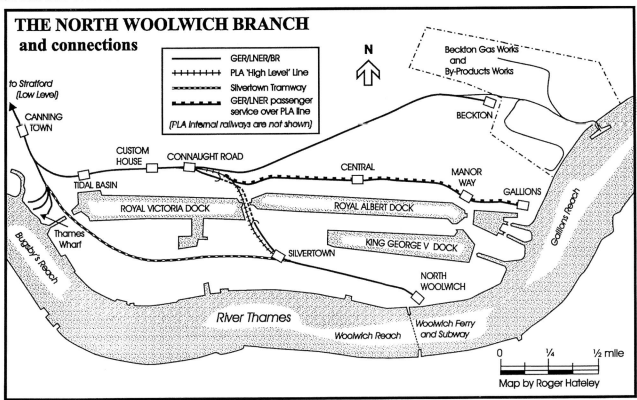

THE NORTH WOOLWICH BRANCH and connections

———————	GER/LNER/BR
+++++++	PLA 'High Level' Line
-×-×-×-×-	Silvertown Tramway
▪▪▪▪▪▪▪	GER/LNER passenger service over PLA line

(PLA internal railways are not shown)

N

Beckton Gas Works and By-Products Works

to Stratford (Low Level)

CANNING TOWN

CUSTOM HOUSE

CONNAUGHT ROAD

CENTRAL

MANOR WAY

GALLIONS

BECKTON

TIDAL BASIN

ROYAL VICTORIA DOCK

ROYAL ALBERT DOCK

Gallions Reach

Thames Wharf

Bugsby's Reach

KING GEORGE V DOCK

SILVERTOWN

NORTH WOOLWICH

River Thames

Woolwich Reach

Woolwich Ferry and Subway

0   ¼   ½ mile

Map by Roger Hateley

A look at the layout of North Woolwich station layout on 28 April 1962. In the left foreground, the North Thames Gas poster and the Regent petrol sign define the period. As for the station itself, for a relatively small passenger terminus it had a large goods yard; apart from Stratford, it was the Great Eastern's only station in the Inner London area which had a goods yard adjacent to the passenger facilities. The goods traffic included domestic coal and general goods, as well as traffic for 'South Woolwich' across the river. The GE at one stage even pointed out that traffic for Woolwich Arsenal and Dockyard should be labelled to North Woolwich 'to avoid the delay and expense of getting through London' (!) Even a cattle pen was provided. The goods facilities were retained until as late as 7 December 1970. The water tower stands behind the locomotive siding. There was also a coal stage in front of the tower, to the right of the engine road. The place did qualify for a coalman at one time, but no train crews were based here. And no doubt the coalman was found other work on the railway and also on the ferry to occupy his time. The left-hand passenger platform is occupied by an LCGB Rail Tour train which had J15 65476 standing tender-first. The Rail Tour was advertised in the railway press: '...to run over various Great Eastern suburban lines which are now dieselised or electrified. The train will leave Liverpool Street at 10.30am and run via Temple Mills, South Tottenham to Palace Gates (reverse), South Tottenham, Stratford to Chingford (reverse), Loughton Branch Junction, Stratford Low Level and North Woolwich (reverse) back to Liverpool Street, arriving at approximately 7.30pm. The train will be hauled by a J15 and possibly by an N7 for part of the journey. Tickets are 15/- (half-fare for children)'.

N7 0-6-2T 69718 on 16 March 1957 – its 29th year as a Stratford engine! – arrives at North Woolwich with the 12.46pm (SO) from Stratford Low Level. The modellers among us will spot the GE disc signal and clearance bar by the right hand rail ahead of the loco. The train is formed of a couple of Quint-Art sets – such was the traffic at lunchtime on Saturdays. As a further guide to the business in this area, the 669 trolleybus route along Albert Road (to the right of the train) ran, at this date, at 5 minute intervals during off-peak periods, 4 minutes at peak times and every 4½ minutes on Sunday afternoons! The desolation of World War II is still apparent – this area, being adjacent to the Royal Docks, was a prime target for the enemy. The proximity of the docks is evidenced by the cranes on the right; given the markings on the ship's funnel among the cranes, it could be one of the Union Castle Line.

We return to Silvertown station, but this picture was taken twelve years later on 13 September 1969. Compare this to our earlier picture – the station nameboard has changed from LNER to BR (ER) style and that on the box has gone from black on white to exactly the opposite. That old mystery vehicle now has an end door but has lost its 'serving hatch'. The sugar refinery and motley collection of factories loom over the scene. The imposing signal box had closed on 24 August 1969 – i.e. some three weeks before this picture was taken – and the signals have already gone. From the date the 'box closed, the Down line became the single line for passenger trains between Custom House and North Woolwich and the Up became bi-directional for freights. The platform we are looking at is therefore not used by passengers.

Above. Still on 13 September 1969, the photographer has turned around to face north-west, and we see that the High Level route between Custom House and Silvertown, which had last been used in April 1966 and had formally been taken out of use in October 1967, had by this time been disconnected. Trains now used the Low Level route which dropped at 1 in 50 into the tunnel under the channel between the Royal Albert Dock and the Royal Victoria Dock. The road on the right is Connaught Road. In the mid-distance on the far left is part of the original route to North Woolwich – the one which opened to passenger traffic in 1847. That section was superseded by the new line via Custom House and Connaught Road which opened in 1855. The old alignment between Rthames Wharf Junction and Silvertown became a 'goods only' line, popularly referred to as the Silvertown Tramway. That tramway served many industrial premises including Silver's works, Keiller's jam factory, Burt Bolton & Haywood's tar factory, Brunner Mond chemical works (where there was a massive explosion and fire in 1917 – over 70 people were killed and many hundreds injured), Venesta's plywood factory, John Knight's Royal Primrose Soap Works, Abram Lyle's sugar factory (which later became the famous Tate & Lyle company), the romantically named Peruvian Guano Works, Plaistow Malt Works and the lyrical Odams Chemical Manure Company. Even as late as 1964 there were no less than 18 private sidings off the tramway, the traffic being serviced from Silvertown Yard.

Below. Connaught Road Swing Bridge – with the road and rail crossings side by side – looking towards Silvertown on 13 September 1969. Swing Bridge No 1 Signal Box used to be located at this point but it was removed in the mid-1930s. When motor traffic increased, it was necessary to install road traffic signals on the road part of the swing bridge.

The Port of London Authority had an extensive internal railway system at the Royal Docks. At its greatest extent the system comprised 70 miles of track, the exchange yard at Custom House had 35 sidings with a combined capacity of some 1,300 wagons, and over twenty PLA locomotives were based there. PLA No.60 was a Hudswell Clarke 0-6-0T (W/No.1254 of 1917) – these Hudswell Clarkes were regarded as the PLA's standard six-coupled locomotives. It is seen approaching Connaught Road Swing Bridge No.2 Signal Box with a rake of meat vans from King George V Dock on 16 March 1957. When the Royal Albert Dock was being connected to the Victoria Dock, the route to North Woolwich was moved for the second time, this time into a tunnel beneath the shipping channel. When the tunnel route was established, the original (now severed) line via the High Level was reconnected by a

joint road/rail swing bridge, and the dock company took over the old route. The dock company installed GER-pattern signals (as seen here); even the 21-lever signal box has a GE look about it. The signals were originally gas lit but were later converted to electric lighting. Passenger and goods trains used the High Level line in emergency, either when the tunnel was flooded – which it was from time to time – or by freight trains which were too heavy for the steep gradients in and out of the tunnel. Whatever the reason or the type of train, movements over the High Level were at severely restricted speeds. *(The PLA's railways is a vast subject – we looked at the system at the Royal Docks in a two-part article in Bylines 3:2 and 3:3 back in 1998)*

Below. Going back to March 1957, PLA No.78, an 'Austerity' type 0-6-0ST, approaches Connaught Road Swing Bridge with vans from the exchange sidings. The loco was built for the War Department in 1943 but came on loan to the Royal Docks in 1946. It was withdrawn from service there in 1959, having been displaced by diesel shunters transferred from Tilbury Docks that summer. The lines coming in on the right are the ex-GE lines from Albert Dock Junction. These had also been transferred to the dock company after the Low Level lines had been brought into use in 1876.

Our journey ends at Stratford Low Level – the train seen here is the 2.52pm North Woolwich-Palace Gates on 23 June 1956. An F5 2-4-2T is on the front of Quint-Art set E86676-80E which was built by R.Y.Pickering & Co Ltd in 1925. The guard checks a few doors ready for 'Right Away'. The bridge carries the ex-GE main lines to Colchester and Norwich. The colour light signals at the platform end are operated by Fork Junction 'box and read towards Channelsea Junction (Left) and Loop Junction (right), though the latter was not a passenger train route. The lamps on the platform are of LNER design.

THE NORTH WOOLWICH LINE AND THE PLA RAILWAYS

29 April 1846: Stratford Eastern Junction-Thames Wharf opened for freight traffic by the Eastern Counties & Thames Junction Railway.

14 June 1847: Thames Wharf line taken over by the Eastern Counties Railway and extended to North Woolwich; hourly passenger services introduced between Bishopsgate and North Woolwich. Stratford West Curve opened.

Late November 1855: New line opened between Thames Wharf Junction and Silvertown (via the soon-to-be-opened Custom House station). The old line became the Silvertown Tramway (freight only) but was later (possibly in the 1880s) severed at its western end, all traffic subsequently being worked via Silvertown.

26 November 1855: Victoria Dock ceremonially opened ('Royal' prefix not added until 1880); internal rail movements undertaken by horses.

26 November 1855: Custom House station opened.

February 1858: Tidal Basin station opened.

1 July 1862: Eastern Counties Railway becomes part of Great Eastern Railway (though the amalgamation wasn't ratified by an Act of Parliament until 7 August).

19 June 1863: Silvertown station opened.

June 1876: New tunnel opened from east of Custom House to west of Silvertown. Old surface line via Connaught Road swing bridge became dock company property.

1879: Locomotive power first used at Victoria Dock.

24 June 1880: Royal Albert Dock ceremonially opened.

3 August 1880: Dock company's passenger branch opened between Albert Dock Junction (near Custom House station) and Central station.

October 1880: Dock company's branch extended from Central station to Gallions (which was originally named Albert Dock station).

April 1881: GER passenger trains introduced between Custom House and Central.

July 1881: Manor Road station (soon renamed Manor Way) opened on the Gallions branch.

July 1881: GER passenger services from Custom House extended to Gallions.

12 December 1886: Original station at Gallions replaced by new station 275 yards to the east.

31 March 1909: Port of London Authority formed.

8 July 1921: Ceremonial opening of the King George V Dock.

6 July 1932: Custom House-Gallions passenger services withdrawn.

30 September 1935 to 28 March 1936: Rail tunnel under the Royal Victoria Dock/Royal Albert Dock junction channel closed for remedial work after it had been discovered that ships passing through the channel were scraping the roof of the tunnel! North Woolwich passenger trains diverted via PLA's 'surface line' over Connaught Road swing bridge.

15 August 1943: Tidal Basin station closed.

1 January 1962: DMUs introduced on North Woolwich line.

18 April 1966: Last reported usage of PLA's 'high level' line across Connaught Road swing *bridge*.

October 1967: Connaught Road swing bridge formally taken out of use (but bridge not dismantled until 1973).

11 January 1969: Saturday passenger services ceased on North Woolwich line.

24 August 1969: Lines between North Woolwich and Custom House became bi-directional – old Down line for passenger trains and old Up line for freight trains.

May 1970: PLA railway system at Royal Docks closed.

7 December 1970: Freight services ceased at North Woolwich.

1981: Royal Docks closed.

13 May 1985: Dalston Junction-North Woolwich electrified; ex-SR Class 416/3 units used.

1986: Silvertown Tramway formally taken out of use.

7 October 1989: Silvertown station renamed Silvertown & London City Airport.

1993: All freight movements on North Woolwich line ceased.

29 May 1994: Stratford-North Woolwich closed for Jubilee Line extension work.

29 October 1995: Line reopened.

Shock, horror… a hefty great 8F in *Bylines*! The stranger in the camp is 48378 of Wellingborough – it is passing through Stratford Low Level with a train of coal hoppers, probably for Beckton to load coke. The date is 30 June 1956. Stratford Eastern Curve to the Colchester main line is to the right. It was taken out of use on 20 July 1969. The large building in the centre is the District Engineer's office which was built in 1938.

A little gem with a very clear message – leading by example is Bagnall 'fireless' 0-4-0, shunting at the Prince Regent Tar Company at Prince Regent's Wharf, Silvertown, on 16 March 1957. The locomotive was built in 1947 (W/No.2851) and came new to the tar works; its predecessor, a small Hibberd 'Planet' diesel, had been destroyed a few years earlier during an air raid. The tar works closed in 1969 and the locomotive was scrapped at the end of that year. Now – just what is being discussed by the men on the steelwork? (Sorry – there are no prizes. This is not a *Bylines* quiz.)

The ICI (Alkali Division) works at Silvertown – these were the old Brunner Mond works – were connected by their own Clyde Wharf and Crescent Wharf on the Thames by means of the Silvertown Tramway. Ten different locomotives saw service at the alkali works over the years. Among them were three 0-4-0 well tanks – one was a Borrows original while the other two were Kerr Stuart versions. BLACK was one of the Kerr Stuart examples. Built in 1917 (W/No.3048) it had worked at ICI's Winnington Works at Northwich before coming to Silvertown in January 1953. This picture was taken on 16 March 1957. The posed nature of the picture reveals that it was taken during an official visit, the locomotives being positioned specially for the photographers in the party. Just eight months later, in November 1957, BLACK was scrapped locally by T.W.Ward. Now, who is going to tell us who the original 'BLACK' was? A director of Brunner Mond, perhaps? It's not a catch question – we really don't know!

Also photographed during the visit to the ICI works on 16 March 1957 was J.B.GANDY (no – we don't know who he was either), a four-wheeled Ruston & Hornsby, W/No.299103 of 1950. ICI closed the Silvertown works in March 1961 and J.B.GANDY was transferred the following month to ICI's Tunstead Works in Derbyshire. It later moved to Hindlow Limeworks where it survived until spring 1982.

FOURUM – the other Caley Pugs

In 1885 a pair of 0-4-2STs were built by the Caledonian Railway at St.Rollox Works. The engines, which were numbered 262 and 263, had been part of an order for ten 0-4-0STs but, while they had been under construction, the two had been altered to 0-4-2STs so that they would be suitable for working the Killin branch which was nearing completion. The engines duly took up their position on the Killin branch but were displaced in the 1890s and eventually finished up on ordinary shunting duties – the sort of duties for which their 0-4-0ST counterparts had been intended. In 1918 the two 0-4-2STs were placed on the Caley's duplicate list as 1262 and 1263. Our upper picture shows the former, looking rather smart in the Caley livery which it retained until withdrawal in 1928. After the grouping it had been designated LMS 15000,

but had not carried that number. The Westinghouse gear had been fitted *circa* 1887 to comply with Board of Trade regulations – as already noted, in those days these 0-4-2STs were passenger engines. The two coal rails atop the bunker were also later additions. Our lower picture shows the other one of the pair (the one-time Caley 263) as LMS 15001. It would seem that the livery had been very recently applied – and most impressive it is too. Note the solid trailing wheels; the trailing axle had side play only and was not radial. Unfortunately, we do not know where either of these pictures were taken, nor the precise dates. If anyone can help us out with those details please let us know. BOTH PHOTOGRAPHS: J.T.RUTHERFORD, THE TRANSPORT TREASURY

Although 15001 looked very smart after having its LMS livery applied, in its later years it suffered from the sort of neglect which most shunting engines had to endure. 15001 was transferred to Inverness in 1933, its principal duties being on the Harbour branch which had previously been the domain of veteran Stroudley ex-Highland 0-6-0T 16119. The picture above is another 'don't know where, don't know when' – we suspect it was taken at Inverness in the 1930s but we would welcome confirmation (or otherwise). Relief at last – the picture below came with a location and date! The location is Inverness (it looks like the south side of the

shed yard but we stand to be corrected) and the date is 9 April 1946. 15001's crew clearly aren't taking any chances with running short of coal – the stuff is even carried on the cab roof. 15001 was withdrawn from Inverness in April 1947. Several of its contemporaries which had been built, as originally intended, as 0-4-0STs survived until well into the 1950s and a few soldiered on until the 1960s. Now – wouldn't these be an ideal subject for a full-length article in *Bylines* magazine? PHOTOGRAPHS: WILLIE HERMISTON, THE TRANSPORT TREASURY (upper); H.C.CASSERLEY (lower)

GOODS ONLY – the Ravenhead branch
Photographs by J.A.Sommerfield; notes by Bryan L.Wilson

The Ravenhead branch at St.Helens was a goods only line which left the St.Helens-Widnes line at the appropriately named Ravenhead Junction and extended for about $1\frac{1}{4}$ miles, serving various industrial premises including several glass works, collieries, a smelting works and the lyrically titled Old Teapot Brick Works. Near the end of the branch was a huge works which eventually became Pilkington's fibreglass factory. This is the rail entrance to the Pilkington's works on the north-west side of Ravenhead Road on 21 August 1971. The lodge is a rather attractive building. The vanfits in the yard are loaded with fibreglass and are awaiting collection by a BR engine which will take them to the marshalling yard at Canal Bridge. The 'Pilkington-style' semaphore signal was operated by the flagman – he lowered the signal and inserted a pin to hold it in position. The signal applied both ways, telling the BR driver that the gates were open to rail traffic and also giving permission to leave the factory.

The signal inside the factory gates warned if the gates were open, but it did not give permission to cross Ravenhead Road outside the factory. That was done in the traditional style by a man with a red flag. On 13 April 1977, 08615 was being flagged through.

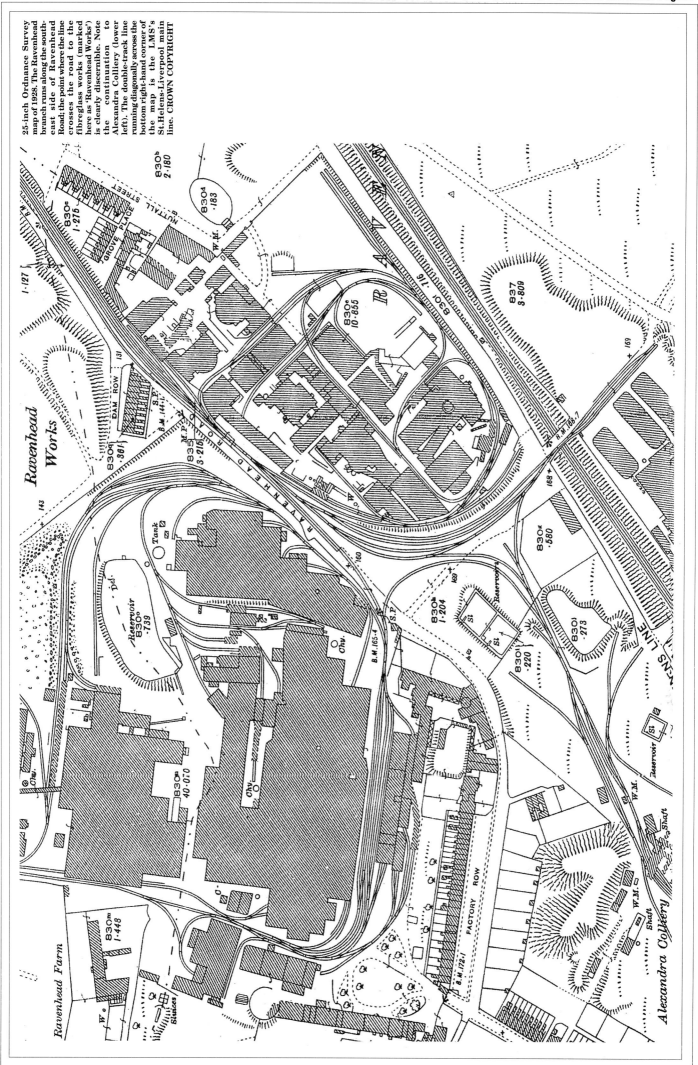

25-inch Ordnance Survey map of 1928. The Ravenhead branch runs along the south-east side of Ravenhead Road; the point where the line crosses the road to the fibreglass works (marked here as 'Ravenhead Works') is clearly discernible. Note the continuation to Alexandra Colliery (lower left). The double-track line running diagonally across the bottom right-hand corner of the map is the LMS's St.Helens-Liverpool main line. CROWN COPYRIGHT

Right. On its way back from the fibreglass factory a train had to descend at 1 in 75 before reaching Marsh's Crossing. This was where the railway crossed Burtonhead Road near its junction with Canal Street. As an aid to getting one's bearings, we are looking east and the bridge in the distance carries the main line between St.Helens Shaw Street and Liverpool Lime Street. The signal box (which closed on 25 February 1979) housed a 15-lever LNW tumbler frame; it also held the staffs for the single lines and had a control phone – as there were no block instruments no other boxes communicated with Marshs' Crossing 'box, so the phone was the only means of controlling operations. The signalman here dealt with the inspector at Canal Bridge and the ground frame at Menzies Crossing. The crossing gates were hand-operated and locked with Black's Locks, the bolt for these being seen on the right-hand side of the third rung from the bottom. The junction signals beyond the box (with their backs towards us) read, as the driver of a westbound train saw them, left-hand for Nuttalls (United Glass Bottle) and Pilkington's Fibreglass, and right-hand for the Eccleston branch (which diverged to our left a short distance behind the photographer). Beyond the signals and just before the overbridge is a parachute water tank. One thing that is not visible in this picture is the other end of the signal box – whereas the name on the end nearest the camera was Marsh's Crossing, the name on the other end was *Marshes* Crossing! You takes yer money and you makes yer choice... Siberia Warehouse on the left was part of Pilkington's Watson Street empire.

Crates of glass were loaded by overhead crane and the doors were always left open to give access to BR vehicles for loading (hence the Siberian conditions in inclement weather). This picture was taken on 20 August 1971.

Below. Ravenhead Junction, 20 August 1971. The line from Pilkington's fibreglass factory comes in over the photographer's left shoulder (figuratively speaking) while the lines heading off to the right of the photographer go to Sherdley Glass Works and, at one time, to the old Sherdley Colliery which closed *circa*

1943. The bridge in the distance takes the railway across Warrington New Road immediately to the north of its junction with Warrington Old Road. In the far distance the 'hills' are mounds of chemical waste which had been left behind when much of the local chemical industry had defected to Widnes in 1905. Since this picture was taken the tips have been levelled and a factory now sits on the site. The smart Ravenhead Junction signal box was built of timber and had a 20-lever frame. It was destroyed by fire on 9 October 1977.

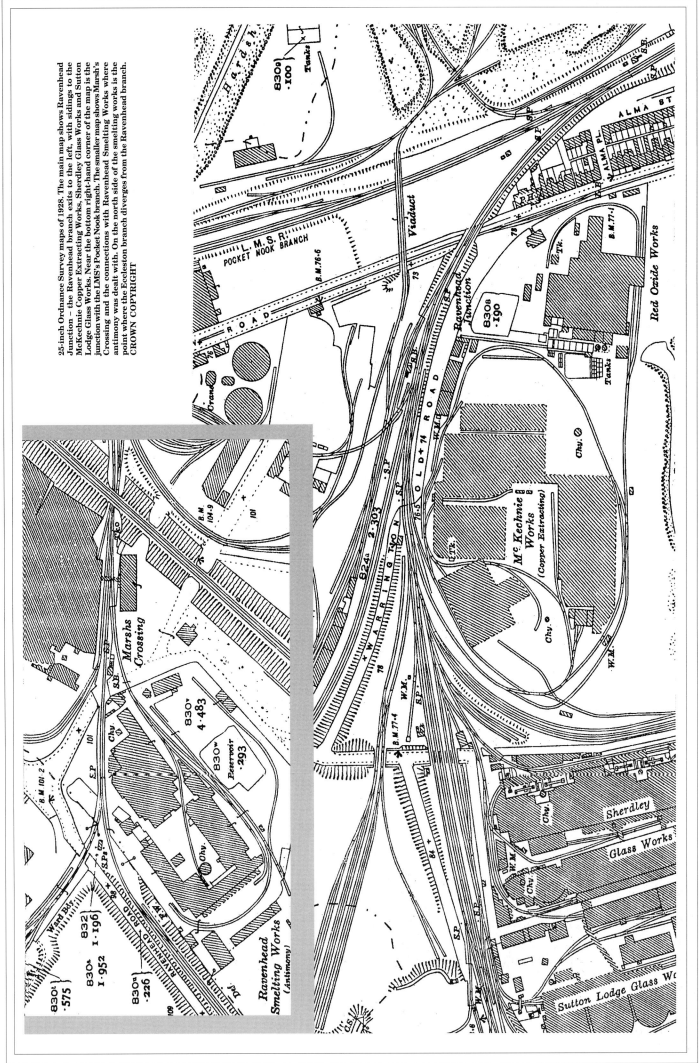

25-inch Ordnance Survey maps of 1928. The main map shows Ravenhead Junction – the Ravenhead branch exits to the left, with sidings to the McKechnie Copper Extracting Works, Sherdley Glass Works and Sutton Lodge Glass Works. Near the bottom right-hand corner of the map is the junction with the LMS's Pocket Nook branch. The smaller map shows Marsh's Crossing and the connections with Ravenhead Smelting Works where antimony was dealt with. On the north side of the smelting works is the point where the Eccleston branch diverges from the Ravenhead branch. CROWN COPYRIGHT

ROGER GOES WEST
Photographs by Roger Palmer

In mid-July 1964 Roger Palmer's travels took him to North Devon and North Cornwall. Lucky chap! On Friday 17 July he visited Bude. This was the last summer of steam on the Bude branch – DMUs took over in September 1964 and remained in charge until the branch closed in October 1966. This is 80037 waiting with the 5.35pm to Halwill.

Saturday 18 July found Roger on the 'withered arm'. This was the scene at Camelford where 80037 arrived with one of the four down trains of the day. Given that the North Cornwall line was on its last legs – closure came in October 1966 – the number of passengers waiting on the up platform is perhaps surprising. Unless those passengers were waiting for the ACE, they would be able to travel no father than Okehampton without changing. Such were the services on the North Cornwall line in 1964.

On Wednesday 22 July Roger visited the Halwill-Torrington line which, by this time, had only two trains over the entire length of the line each way on weekdays. This is 41283 at Hole, the first station out of Halwill. The train is the 10.38am Halwill-Torrington.

The next station along the line from Hole was Hatherleigh, where 41283 took on water. The train was timed to take 84 minutes for the 20½-mile journey from Halwill to Torrington. This picture was taken on the same day as the one above (22 July 1964), so it is a 'last summer of passenger services' picture as the Halwill-Torrington trains were withdrawn as from 1 March 1965.

CONNEL FERRY BRIDGE
Contentious bridge tolls – a touch too much
Notes by 'Our Wullie'

A fine view of the Connel Ferry bridge taken from the south bank of Loch Etive in June 1964. Going back to 24 August 1903, the structure was inspected for the Board of Trade by Major Yorke. In his inspection report he noted that the bridge was '...formed of two steel cantilevers resting on granite piers forming a single span of 500ft, while the total length of the bridge platform is 735ft. The bridge is said to have the longest railway span in the world, with the exception of the Forth Bridge. The clearway above water level is 52ft. At each end of the steel structure there are three arched spans of 38ft 6in'. In view of the then-unconventional nature of the bridge's construction it was submitted to stringent tests which included the passage of a train comprising three tender engines, five tank engines and four large bogie wagons (loaded) – a total weight of 730 tons or 1.75 tons per lineal foot. Five test runs were made and the deflections recorded were negligible. PHOTOGRAPH: J.KIRKE; THE TRANSPORT TREASURY

Following the abandonment of a scheme for a main line railway from Connel Ferry to Inverness, the Callander & Oban Railway looked instead at the idea of a $27^1/_2$-mile branch line from Connel Ferry to Ballachulish. Although the branch line scheme was more modest, it was not without its difficulties. The major difficulty was that the line would have to cross Loch Etive, immediately to the north of Connel Ferry. The most obvious point at which to bridge the loch was near its entrance where it narrowed to 690ft, but the narrowing of the channel and the presence of a rock bar at that point resulted in very strong currents, known as the Falls of Lora. Further evidence of the problematical currents in the area was seen in the name Connel – this derived from the Gaelic *coingheall* which means whirlpool. The currents effectively ruled out the use of staging for the construction of intermediate piers in mid-channel so, whatever type of bridge was planned, it would have to have a very lengthy central span.

The C&O's answer was a cantilever bridge, the steelwork of which could be built out over the water without the need for staging. The consulting engineer

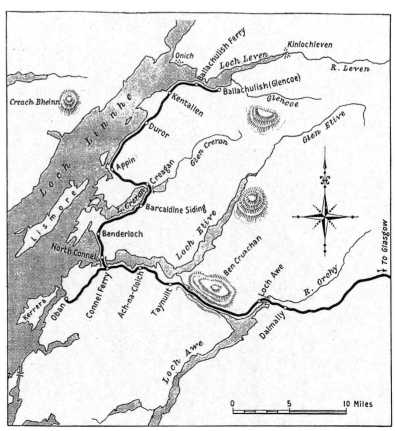

Callander and Oban Railway

Secretarys Office.

58 Bath Street Glasgow.

30th August 1913.

Sir,

Connel Ferry Bridge.

Under the Callander & Oban Railway Act 1896 the Company were empowered to construct an extension of their Railway from Connel Ferry to Ballachulish it was necessary to Bridge Loch Etive and for that purpose a Bridge of considerable demensions suitable for vehicular, passenger and other traffic was erected.

Lately the inhabitants of the District petitioned the Lorn District Committee of the Argyll County Council to endeavour to arrange with the Company for the opening of that portion of the Bridge.

It has been suggested that the Callander & Oban Railway Coy., make provision to allow motor cars to cross the Bridge on their own wheels and that it is proposed to place gates across the new appoach road at each end of the Bridge as shewn on the plan.

I send herewith two plans showing the proposed works.

These gates could only be opened by a staff which would be looked in an instrument placed in a hut adjoining the gate at the north side of the bridge. This staff would be controlled by an electric lock in conjunction with the tablet instruments at Connel Fer./ West Box and Benderloch Stations, which regulate the railway traffic, and could only be taken out of the instrument when the section of the railway between Connel Ferry and Benderloch Stations is clear of railway traffic.

The working would be as follows:-

When the tablet is withdrawn from the tablet instruments at either Connel Ferry West Box or Benderloch Station for the passing of a train the staff for controlling the gates would be locked in the instrument in the hut and the gates would be secured so that no road traffic could get on to the bridge.

If the staff for controlling the gates is withdrawn from the instrument the tablet for controlling the trains could not be removed from either of the tablet instruments at Connel Ferry West Box or Benderloch Station, so that no train could be admitted on to the section when the section is occupied by road vehicles.

A man would be placed in the hut to control the working of the staff instrument and open and close the gates as required, and there would be bell communication between the gate at the south end of the bridge and the hut.

Assuming that the railway is clear to allow of vehicles passing across the bridge and that there are vehicles at the north end of the bridge waiting to pass over to the south side, the gate at the north end would be opened with the staff by the man from the hut and after the vehicles are admitted on to the railway the gate would be relocked. The man with the staff would then accompany the vehicles over the bridge to the south side, and after unlocking the gate at the south side he would allow the vehicles to pass through. He would then relock the gate, walk back over the bridge and place the staff in the instrument in the hut. The staff could not be removed from the gates until they have been relocked.

When vehicles are approaching the bridge from the south side the man in the hut will be advised by the bell being rung, and having walked across the bridge would open the gate, admit the traffic on to the railway, lock the gate, and return to the north side with the vehicles, and having seen them through the gate on the north side return the staff to the instrument after having locked the gate.

The Directors of the Company are making an inspection of the line on 8th September and it would be a favour if the Board of Trade could give an indication before that time whether they would be disposed to agree to the proposal.

I am,

Sir,

Your obedient Servant,

Andw Crosbie

The Assistant Secretary,

Railway Department,

Board of Trade,

L O N D O N.

---

engaged for the project was Sir John Wolfe Barry and the contractors were the Arrol Bridge & Roofing Company which, under the guidance of William Arrol, had built the Forth Bridge, the only other significant cantilever railway bridge in Britain. The construction of Connel Ferry bridge started in 1898 and was completed in June 1903. The structure incorporated 2,600 tons of steelwork.

The railway line across the bridge was ceremonially opened on Friday 21 August 1903 and public traffic commenced between Connel Ferry and Ballachulish the following Monday. In common with the C&O's main line, the branch was worked by the Caledonian Railway.

It might be thought that the new railway would be regarded as a boon by those living in the area, but there was a major bone of contention concerning Connel Ferry bridge. A footpath-cum-roadway had been built alongside the railway on the bridge and the C&O considered that, as it had paid for the construction of the bridge, it should be able to recoup some money from users of the footpath/roadway. With this in mind the C&O offered the footpath to Argyll County Council for an annual rental of £800, but the council considered the sum excessive and declined. The C&O proved similarly inflexible and kept the footpath closed to the public. The only way for the public to cross the bridge was by train for which the charge was 2d – the equivalent of the fare for a two-mile journey, even though the distance between Connel Ferry and North Connel stations was a mere ³/₄-mile.

The C&O's stance incurred the wrath of many individuals and local organisations, but the company wouldn't budge. However, in July 1909 the Caledonian (the working company) introduced the 'Connel Bus' between Connel Ferry station and either North Connel or Benderloch station. The 'bus' was a charabanc which had been converted to run on rails (see Railway Bylines 5:6, May 2000) and, importantly, it was designed to haul one or two 'car trailers' – these were flat wagons on to which cars could be loaded. The cost of taking a car across Loch Etive on the 'car trailer' was a massive 15/0d (equivalent to roughly £45 these days – honest!) but, despite this, in the summer months the service was very popular and motorists were often faced with long waits.

Local authorities and various organisations continued to pressurise the C&O to make the roadway on the bridge available for all and sundry, but yet again the company resisted. However, in 1913 a local chap – one Macalpine Downie – applied to operate a chain ferry between Connel Ferry and North Connel, and the C&O, faced with this threat of competition, made a spectacular U-turn. The railway company purchased land for improving the road approaches to the bridge and also lashed out £2,022 on adapting the footpath for motor vehicles. But just when the local motorists were starting to think that their lot was about to improve, the C&O announced its proposed bridge tolls:15/0d for a single crossing and 22/6d return. Predictably, this prompted another outcry.

Uncharacteristically mindful of public opinion, the C&O reduced its charges to 7/6d for a single journey in a two-seater car or 10/0d for larger cars or commercial vehicles. These revised tolls were still very expensive indeed, but the C&O was fully aware that the only alternative for road users was a 35-mile detour which, in winter, was often snowbound.

The date of the opening of the bridge to road traffic has usually been stated to be 22 June 1914 (we quoted that date ourselves in our earlier article about the 'Connel Bus') but, as will be seen from the accompanying copies of recently discovered paperwork, the formal announcement in the *Oban Times* gives a date of 16 October 1914. Whatever the date, the opening of the roadway rendered the 'Connel Bus' redundant and it was withdrawn from service.

The C&O's bridge tolls continued to cause much discontent. As John Thomas explains in his excellent *The Callander & Oban Railway:* 'The bridge built up a massive fund of ill-will for the railway. Pleas and protests were useless. The man in the toll box was a law unto himself. Anything exhibiting a hackney plate he refused at any price. A shepherd could take his flock across, but he had to lead the beasts one at a time. A funeral cortege could not cross as such – coffins had to be removed from the hearses and carried across the bridge on payment of the appropriate toll; alternatively, the coffin could be taken by train, again on payment of the specified rate'.

In 1930 a new main road was opened through Glencoe. This meant that motorists going to or from the Ballachulish area now had an alternative route free of the swingeing bridge tolls and, inevitably, the road traffic crossing the bridge declined. The new road also had an effect on rail traffic as many of the railway's freight customers in the Ballachulish area also found the road through Glencoe more convenient.

The bridge tolls for commercial vehicles were reduced during the war, but it was 1 June 1954 before there was a reduction in tolls for *all* bridge users. The cost of taking a car across was now 4/0d for cars under 11hp, 5/0d for cars between 11 and 16hp, or 5/0d for cars over 16hp. This might have been a huge reduction, but crossing the bridge still wasn't cheap

Caledonian Railway Company
Solicitor's Office
302, Buchanan Street,
Glasgow, 4th June 1914.

TELEGRAMS: "CALSOL, GLASGOW."
TELEPHONE: "3603 DOUGLAS."

Sir,

Connel Ferry Bridge.
R. 6618.

I have your letter of 29th ultimo with enclosures.

While it is the case that section 8 of the Callander & Oban Railway Act 1896 contemplates agreement between the Railway Company and the Road Authority as to the terms and conditions restrictions and regulations affecting the use of Connel Ferry Bridge by other than railway traffic the section also contemplates a contribution by the Road Authority towards the cost of construction and maintenance of the bridge and approaches to serve the purposes of traffic other than railway traffic.

As the Road Authority have contributed nothing to the cost of construction and do not propose to contribute anything to the cost of maintenance and as the provisions of section 8 are permissive and not obligatory neither the Company nor the Road Authority are to suggest any agreement under section 8.

The local Road Authority is the Lorn District Committee of the County Council of Argyllshire, and they have been communicated with in the matter and are aware of what is proposed.

It is also to be noted that section 8 of the Act of 1896 seems to enact specially and differently in regard to tolls and charges for the use of the bridge by traffic other than railway traffic. The section specially empowers the Company to levy such tolls and other charges as may be approved by the Board of Trade. It is in view of this provision that the list of tolls has been submitted to you.

The Company is prepared to justify the tolls proposed. Particulars of them have been supplied to the Clerk of the Lorn District Committee, Mr William Ironside, Writer, Oban, and are being sent also to Messrs Macandrew Wright and Murray, W.S. 9 Albyn Place, Edinburgh, Law Agents for the Lochnell Estate.

I am, Sir,

Your obedient Servant,

Solicitor,
Callander & Oban Railway Company

The Assistant Secretary,
(Railway Department)
Board of Trade,
7, Whitehall Gardens,
LONDON.   S.W.

THE SCOTTISH AUTOMOBILE CLUB.

Secretary's Office,

163, West George Street,

Glasgow.

8th June, 1914.

The Secretary,
     The Board of Trade,
          London.

Sir,

                Callander & Oban Railway - Connel
                        Ferry Bridge

        I am instructed to communicate with you on the
subject of the rates for passage of motor vehicles over the
vehicular roadway just completed by the Railway Company
on the Railway Bridge spanning Loch Etive at Connel Ferry.
The club understands that it is proposed to levy tolls on
motor vehicles equivalent to the amounts presently charged
for conveyance of such by special truck service, viz., 15/-
per single journey and 22/6 for a double journey in the same
day in respect of motor cars and 7/6 per single journey in respect of motor cycles with side cars, and that these rates
are presently before your Board for approval The Club
respectfully submits that the proposed charges are excessive
and should be very considerably modified. They are unaware
of any bridge toll - public or private - in the Kingdom which
is more than a mere fraction of the rates suggested in this
instance.

        The Club believes that the increased facility for
crossing Loch Etive which the new roadway will afford will
encourage many local and touring motorists to avail them-
selves of it. They are satisfied, however, that at the

proposed tolls many who would otherwise use the crossing
will refrain from doing so, but that if the inducement
of reasonable and lower charges are offered a very
largely increased traffic will ensue. Many motorists temporarily resident in Oban will be induced to make a circular tour via Connel, Ballachulish and Glencoe, while
many others who presently travel north and south via
Glencoe will include Oban and Connel in their itinerary.
It appears to the Club that rates one half of those proposed would be adequate, but they would respectfully suggest that if in fixing the rates some regard be given
to the cost of making and working the roadway, to the in
creased traffic which may reasonably be expected, and to
the net income from the superseded service, an equitable
basis of rating might be arrived at.

        The Club would further submit that in fixing the
tolls some consideration should be given to light cars and
cyclecars, of which many have in recent months been put
upon the road, and the manufacture of which is likely to
become an important branch of the motor industry. It
occurs to them to suggest that the car and driver be rated
apart from passengers (passengers bearing a somewhat larger
proportion of the whole than under present rates) and that
two seaters
    /be rated differently from four or more seated cars.

        I refer you to the Callander & Oban Railway Act,
1896, Sect. 8 in respect of the provision of roadways, and
would emphasise the view that in the mind of the road user
and of the public generally the use of a bridge road is not
equivalent to the provision of railway and truck service,
and the charges for the one would not be considered con-
sonant with those for the other.

        The Club has in its membership over 2,300 owners
of motor vehicles in Scotland and one of its objects
and functions is the encouragement of touring in Scotland.
The Club is in association with the Royal Automobile
Club whose members and associates number over 39,700, and
in all matters relating to roads and touring in Scotland
is its recognised and authorised representative. Many
of the members and associates of both bodies tour largely
throughout Scotland, and the subject matter under
discussion is of importance and interest to them.
A considerable number of the members of this and of the
Royal Automobile Club are resident permanently or
temporarily in Argyllshire and are specially affected
and interested, while to the hirers of motor vehicles
in Oban the matter is extremely important.

                                I am,

                                     Sir,

                                Your obedient Servant,

                                (Sd) Robert J. Smith.

                                          Secy.

– 4/0d in 1954 is equivalent to £3.20 today, and let's not forget that this was for a trip of only a little over 350 yards! As can be seen from the accompanying documentation there was still considerable discontent with the bridge tolls, but there were no changes until after the closure of the Connel Ferry-Ballachulish branch line on 28 March 1966. Before agreeing to the closure the Department of Transport had stipulated that the bridge should be devoted entirely to road traffic and that the tolls should be abolished. This they were, and it finally brought an end to a 63-year-long source of intense local discontent.

AUTOMOBILE ASSOCIATION & MOTOR UNION

FANUM HOUSE
WHITCOMB St COVENTRY St
LONDON.

The Assistant Secretary,
Railway Department,
Board of Trade,
Whitehall, S.W.

9th June, 14.

Sir,

The attention of the Association has been called to the opening of the bridge at Connel Ferry (Argyll) to vehicular traffic, and the prohibitory charges which the railway company propose to make in respect of the passage of motor vehicles over the bridge.

The Association understands that the Callender and Oban Railway Company have now come to an arrangement with the Argyll County Council by which the road shall be opened to vehicular traffic under Section 8 of the Callender and Oban Railway Act, but in as much as the proposed charges are 15/- single journey and 22/6 return journey for four seater cars, and 12/6 single journey and 22/6 return journey for two seater cars, it will be seen that the charges are such as to effectively negative the value of the opening of the bridge in question.

It is anticipated that the bridge will be used by a large number of motorists during the touring season, and having regard to all the circumstances it is the view of the Association that the proposed charges are extremely unreasonable.   In view of the fact that the approval of the Board is necessary before such charges can be imposed I am desired to enquire whether the Board will give this matter consideration with a view to securing the use of the bridge for motor car traffic at much smaller charges.

I am, Sir,
Your obedient Servant,

Caley 0-4-4T 55224 comes off the south end of Connel Ferry bridge with the 3.47pm Ballachulish-Oban train on 14 May 1960. PHOTOGRAPH: W.A.C.SMITH

IWH

Argyll County Council
Lorn District Committee.

William Ironside.
JOHN D. SUTHERLAND,
SOLICITOR, OBAN.
DISTRICT CLERK.

Oban, 12th June, 1914.

The Assistant Secretary,
    Railway Department,
        Board of Trade,
            7, Whitehall Gardens,
                London, S.W.

Sir,

R. 6765.

Referring to your letter of the 5th inst., I am
directed by the Lorn District Committee to take the follow:
ing objections to the proposals made by the Caledonian Rail:
way Company with reference to Connel Ferry Railway Bridge.

1. Objection is taken to the restriction of the hours
during which the Bridge can be used for vehicular and passen:
ger traffic. Most of the passenger traffic will be probably
after 8 p.m., - at least during summer. One object in wish:
ing to have the Bridge open at night is on account of the
medical needs of Benderloch.

2. The District Committee think that animals other than
led animals should be allowed to cross the bridge.

3. The District Committee have not yet received an offic:
ial list of the tolls proposed to be charged, though they have
got an unofficial list, and in the District Committee's opinion
these tolls are far too high.

4. The Committee suggest that the Bridge should be open
for cattle or sheep being driven across, and they would have

no objection to the old ferry rates, which were 10d. a score
for sheep, 8d. a score for lambs up to a year old, and 4d. each
for cattle.

When you supply a list of the tolls proposed, the
Committee will state in detail the tolls they think should
be charged.

I am, Sir,

Your obedient Servant,

[signature]

District Clerk.

ALL LETTERS TO BE ADDRESSED TO THE SOLICITOR.

Caledonian Railway Company
Solicitor's Office
302, Buchanan Street.
Glasgow, 13th July 1914.

TELEGRAMS: "CALBOL, GLASGOW."
TELEPHONE: "3603 DOUGLAS."

Sir,

Connel Ferry Railway Bridge.

I have your letter of 10th instant and note that the
Board propose to appoint Sheriff A. O. M. Mackenzie to hold
an Inquiry into this matter.

It is perhaps proper at this stage that I should make
it clear on behalf of the Callander and Oban and Caledonian
Railway Companies that the Inquiry to be held will not in
their view be of the nature of an arbitration, the result of
which they will be bound to abide by.

The Railway Companies consider that it is entirely in
their discretion whether or not the Connel Ferry Railway
Bridge be made available for the purposes of traffic other
than railway traffic, and that they are at liberty to close
the bridge against non-railway traffic if, in their opinion,
their interests should render such a course desirable.

I am, Sir,

Your obedient Servant,

Hugh R. Buchanan

The Assistant Secretary,
    Board of Trade,
        (Railway Department),
            7, Whitehall Gardens,
                L O N D O N. S.W.

Below. The southern approach. PHOTOGRAPH: E.P.SUGDEN

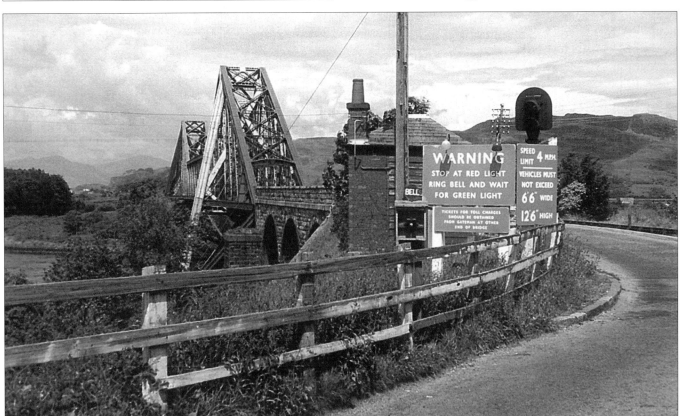

Letters in this case should be
addressed:—
"The Secretary,
Highlands and Islands
(Medical Service) Board,
4a St. Andrew Square,
Edinburgh,"
and the following number should be
quoted :—
14/891.

HIGHLANDS AND ISLANDS

(MEDICAL SERVICE) BOARD,

EDINBURGH

IMMEDIATE.

27th July, 1914.

Sir,

I beg to inform you that my Board have recently had
under consideration proposals for the improvement of medical
and nursing services in the County of Argyll.   A Committee
of the Board visited Oban on the 20th instant and, in the
course of an enquiry into the proposals received from the
Lorn District of the County, the conditions under which it
is proposed that the Connel Ferry Railway Bridge should be
available for non-railway traffic were brought to their
notice.

From the point of view of the medical and nursing
services in the district the Board are in full sympathy with
the Lorn District Committee in their representation that the
bridge should not be closed at 8 p.m. and the Board suggest
that, if it is still found to be expedient to close the bridge
at that hour to the general public, doctors and nurses in the
execution of their duty and messengers conveying medicines
to patients should be allowed to go and come over the bridge
at any hour.

The Board would further suggest for the consideration of the Board of Trade and the Railway Companies concerned that, in the interests of a fuller medical service
for the Benderloch district, no charge for the use of the
bridge should be made in respect of motor or other vehicles
used by doctors and nurses in visiting patients, or, alternatively, that the rates in respect of such traffic should
be greatly reduced.

A copy of this letter has been sent to the
Caledonian Railway Company, the Callender and Oban Railway
Company and the Lorn District Committee.

I am, Sir,

Your obedient Servant,

The Assistant Secretary,
   Railway Department,
      Board of Trade,
         7, Whitehall Gardens,
            L O N D O N, S.W.

Cars could cross the bridge only when there were no trains, but given the infrequency of the services on the Ballachulish branch – for much of the 1950s there were just four passenger trains each way on weekdays and an additional one on Saturdays – this did not present too much of an obstacle to road movements. This picture gives a good view of the guard rail alongside the track. PHOTOGRAPH: MICHAEL E.WARE

CALEDONIAN RAILWAY COMPANY.
CALLANDER AND OBAN RAILWAY COMPANY.

Use of Connel Ferry Railway Bridge by Non-Railway Traffic.

NOTICE IS HEREBY GIVEN,

THAT on and after 16TH OCTOBER, 1914, the CONNEL FERRY RAILWAY BRIDGE of the CALLANDER AND OBAN RAILWAY COMPANY will be OPEN for use by other than railway traffic to the extent and on the conditions undernoted :—

1. The bridge will be open daily (Sundays included), from one hour before sunrise until one hour after sunset, but in no case before 8 a.m. or after 8 p.m.

2. No commercial vehicle of any sort shall be allowed to use the bridge with the exception of commercial vehicles travelling empty on their own wheels for purposes of delivery or repair.

3. No animals shall be allowed to cross the bridge unless led singly.

4. No vehicle of more than 3½ tons axle weight shall be allowed to cross.

5. No explosives shall be taken across the bridge by any person or in any vehicle.

6. The speed of vehicles on the bridge must not exceed four miles per hour.

7. Any vehicle breaking down on the bridge or approaches shall be removed forthwith by the owner or person in charge, failing which the Company may do so at the expense of such owner or person in charge and without incurring any liability for any damage so resulting.

8. The use of the bridge by other than railway traffic is subordinate to its use by railway traffic, and the Company will not be liable in respect of any delay to traffic other than railway traffic which may be caused in the interests or on account of railway traffic.

9. All persons using the bridge and approaches must obey the instructions of the Company's representative in charge.

10. The Company will not be liable in respect of any accident to any person using the bridge and approaches, but all such persons shall be held to use the same at their own risk so far as regards the nature of the construction or equipment of the bridge, or roadway, or accesses. The Railway Company shall not by virtue of this regulation be exempt from liability which may arise from negligence in the maintenance of the bridge, or roadway, or accesses, or from the negligence of the Company's servants.

11. For the use of the bridge as above provided, the Company are authorised to charge the tolls undernoted. The tolls due shall be paid to the Company's representative and a voucher obtained before the bridge is entered on.

CLASS OF TRAFFIC.	TOLLS.
Passengers (including driver of each vehicle), whether on foot, mounted, or driven.	2d each.
Dogs,	2d each.
Perambulators,	1/- ,,
Bicycles,	6d ,,
Tricycles,	1/- ,,
Motor Bicycles,	2/- ,,
,, ,, (with side car or trailer),	4/- ,,
Motor Tricycles,	4/- ,,
Horse (mounted or led),	5/- ,,
Cattle and other animals led singly :—	
Bull,	5/- ,,
Cow,	4/- ,,
Sheep or Pig,	2/- ,,
Motor passenger vehicles having seats for not more than two persons inside the body of the car,	7/6 ,,
Motor passenger vehicles having seats for more than two persons inside the body of the car	10/- ,,
Horse-drawn vehicles, two-wheeled (including horses drawing the vehicles),	5/- ,,
Horse-drawn vehicles, four-wheeled (including horses drawing the vehicles),	7/6 ,,
Commercial motor vehicles travelling empty on their own wheels for purposes of delivery or repair,	10/- ,,

(Signed) J. BLACKBURN,
Secretary,
Caledonian Railway Company.

(Signed) AND. CROSBIE,
Secretary,
Callander and Oban Railway Company.

The Board of Trade hereby signify their approval of the above regulations and tolls.

Signed by order of the Board of Trade this 12th day of October, 1914. 432

(Signed) W. F. MARWOOD,
An Assistant Secretary to the Board of Trade.

From the *Oban Times*, 17 October 1914.

(Copy). R. 6992.

CALLANDER & OBAN RAILWAY COMPANY

CONNEL FERRY BRIDGE

TOLLS proposed for the use of Connel Ferry Bridge by traffic other than railway traffic, as proposed by J. Macalpine-Downie

Class of Traffic	TOLLS
Passenger (including driver of each vehicle)....	2d. each whether on foot, mounted or driven.
Dogs........................	2d. each
Perambulators.................	1/- "
Bicycles......................	5d. "
Tricycles.....................	1/6 "
Motor Bicycles................	2/6 "
Do.......(with side car or trailer)........	3/6 "
Motor Tricycle................	3/6 "
Horses (mounted or led)........	2/- "
Cattle and other animals led singly............	2/- "
Motor or horse-drawn vehicles, and traders vans	5/-. If returning same day 7/6.
Dog-cart or farmer's trap.....................	
Motor or horse-drawn passenger vehicle seating more than two persons....................	7/6. If returning same day 10/6 for the first two years after that 5/- and 7/6.

The charges announced by Mr.Macalpine Downie for his proposed chain ferry.

Connel Ferry Bridge Tolls

Note of a meeting held at Berkeley Square House on Thursday 25th February,1954

Present:

Mr.E.W.Godfrey (Chairman)   Mr.A.J.Pearson Chief Officer (Special
Mr.C.R.Bowler   Duties) B.T.C.
Mr.A.E.V.Robbins   Mr.A.Stewart Assistant to Chief Region-
Mr.C.S.C.Bridge   al Officer Scottish Region,
                               British Railways
                             Mr.G.D.Fleming Assistant to Chief
                               Officer (Administration)
                               B.T.C.

The meeting was called in accordance with the Minister's suggestion in the final paragraph of his letter of 16th November, 1953, to Sir John Benstead to discuss the possibility of some reduction in the Connel Ferry Bridge tolls in the interests of industry, agriculture and tourism.

Mr. Pearson said that the Commission would be prepared to reduce the tolls to the extent indicated in the attached memorandum dated 23rd February, 1954, but were unable to offer more as the use of the bridge by road traffic was closely linked with the future of the Ballachulish line and any further loss of revenue would raise in an acute form the question of the closing of the branch.

After discussion, particularly as to whether any further help could be given to agriculture and industry, it was agreed that the Commission would consider whether any further offer could be made and would write to the Department.

Mr. Bowler undertook to tell the Private Office of this arrangement.

In view of the setting up under the Transport Act, 1953, in the comparatively near future, of the Scottish railway authority which will have to deal with the question of the future of the Ballachulish branch line it seemed to the Ministry's officials to be undesirable to press the matter any further at the present stage.

FR.9511   MINISTRY OF WAR TRANSPORT

                                           9th March, 1942.

Sir,

CONNEL FERRY RAILWAY BRIDGE

In pursuance of paragraph 1 of the London Midland & Scottish Railway (Connel Ferry Bridge) Order, 1942, the Minister of War Transport hereby approves the following tolls for the use of this Bridge, subject to the provisions of Section 9 of the Callander & Oban Railway Act, 1896, and any other statutory provisions conferring exemption from tolls upon Government traffic:-

(a) the tolls in operation at the date hereof other than the toll of 6/- each from Commercial Motor Vehicles travelling empty on their own wheels for purposes of delivery or repair;

(b) the following tolls for Motor Goods Vehicles:-
Unladen weight not exceeding 1 ton - each 4/- plus 6d. per ton of merchandise carried.
"   " exceeding 1 ton but not exceeding 2½ tons each 6/- plus 6d per ton of merchandise carried
"   " exceeding 2½ tons - each 10/- plus 6d per ton of merchandise carried.

I am, Sir,
Your obedient Servant,

(SGD.) SIDNEY J. PAGE

The President,
London, Midland & Scottish
Railway Company,
Euston Station,

BRITISH TRANSPORT COMMISSION

Schedule of tolls for use of Connel Ferry Railway Bridge by non-railway traffic

Class of Traffic

Persons (including driver of each vehicle), whether on foot, mounted or driven	each	2d.
Bicycles	each	4d.
Motor Bicycles	each	1/3d.
Motor Bicycles (with side car or trailer)	each	2/6d.
Motor Tricycles	each	2/6d.
Horses, whether on foot or in road vehicles	each	1/-
Bulls, " " " " " "	each	1/-
Cows, " " " " " "	each	9d.
Sheep and Pigs, whether on foot or in road vehicles	each	6d.
Horse-drawn Vehicles (and horse drawing the vehicle)	each	3/-
Motor Passenger Vehicles:-		
under 11 h.p.	each	4/-
11 to 16 h.p.	each	5/-
over 16 h.p.	each	6/-
Motor Caravans (Private)	each	6/-
Trailer Caravans	each	6/-
Trailer (luggage)	each	3/-
Motor Buses or Charabancs	each	10/-
Funeral Hearses	each	7/6d.
Motor Goods Vehicles:-		
Unladen weight not exceeding 1 ton - each 4/- plus 6d. per ton of merchandise carried.		
" " exceeding 1 ton but not exceeding 2½ tons - each 6/- plus 6d. per ton of merchandise carried.		
" " " 2½ tons - each 10/- plus 6d. per ton of merchandise carried.		
Motor Tractors	each	6/-
Trailers attached to motor goods vehicles or to tractors - each 6/- plus 6d. per ton of merchandise carried.		

Exceptional charges for Permanent Local Residents living within the following area, viz.,

On North Side of Bridge

Area bounded by Loch Linnhe (West),Kinlochleven, Loch Leven (North), Lochetivehead, Loch Etive (East)

On South Side of Bridge

Area bounded by Oban to Crinan (West), Loch Awe (East), Ardrishaig (South)

	Season Tickets Annual rates		
	£.	s.	d.
Persons		7.	6.
Bicycles		12.	6.
Motor Bicycles	1.	5.	0.
Motor Bicycles (with side car)	1.	10.	0.
Motor cars -			
under 11 h.p.	2.	10.	0.
11 to 16 h.p.	3.	0.	0.
over 16 h.p.	3.	10.	0.
Local retailers' delivery vans, local merchants' delivery vans, local tradesmen's vans (conveying workmen, tools and materials) and local traders' lorries with loads not exceeding 40 cwts.	5.	5.	0.

Exceptional charges for Temporary Residents within the area defined above

	One week			One month			Two months			Three months		
	£.	s.	d.	£.	s.	d.	£.	s.	d.	£.	s.	d.
Persons											7.	6.
Motor cars - under 11 h.p.	1.	0.	0.	1.15.	0.		2.	2.	6.	2.	10.	0.
- 11-16 h.p.	1.	0.	0.	2.	5.	0.	2.	12.	6.	3.	0.	0.
- over 16 h.p.	1.	0.	0.	2.15.	0.		3.	2.	6.	3.	10.	0.
Motor Bicycles		7.	6.		-			-		1.	5.	0.
Motor Bicycles with side car	15.				-			-		1.	10.	0.
Bicycles	2.	6.			-			-			12.	6.

For goods or things not specified in this Schedule of tolls the British Transport Commission may make such reasonable charges as they think fit.

The new tolls, introduced in 1954.

BRITISH TRANSPORT COMMISSION

222 MARYLEBONE ROAD,

LONDON, N.W. 1

Telephone : Ambassador 7711

Our ref.: P/12000.54
Your ref.: RC 6/4/02

August 26th, 1954.

E.W. Godfrey, Esq.,
    Ministry of Transport and Civil Aviation,
      Berkeley Square House,
        London, W.1.

Dear Godfrey,

<u>Connel Ferry Bridge</u>

Since receiving your letter of June 2nd, we have been considering whether it would be possible to make any more concessions in toll charges over the Connel Ferry Bridge, and have come to the conclusion that there is no justification for doing so.

Our Chief Regional Manager in Scotland is satisfied that the interests of agriculture and forestry are not prejudiced by the bridge tolls. For example, for three out of four Forestry Commission forests in the area a more direct route is available via Glencoe for traffic by road to the industrial areas to the east and south.

There is no heavy industry apart from the Bonawe Quarries. This concern formerly sent most of its output in its own steamers to Glasgow and it is only recently that they have begun to supply material for road maintenance in Argyllshire and for electricity schemes in the area. The latest representations may arise from this development.

Even if the tolls were having a restrictive effect on industry, it is difficult to see what we could do about it. You will appreciate that any revenue we deliberately sacrifice here must be made good elsewhere. In addition we should be weakening the case for retaining railway services in this area at all and the Bridge Tolls Committee would no doubt prefer the tolls to having the branch closed altogether.

What Major McCallum and the Bridge Committee seem really to be asking is that the Commission should subsidise road transport to and from the Appin Peninsula. We do not think it is any part of the Commission's responsibilities to do so.

The foregoing is, of course, for your own information.

May I leave you to send a tactful reply to Major McCallum? If, on the other hand, you want any more information from us, we shall be glad to help.

Yours sincerely,

A. J. Pearson.

CHIEF ADMINISTRATIVE OFFICER

Below. **A passenger's view – a car waits while a Ballachulish-bound train crosses the bridge on 19 April 1952. PHOTOGRAPH: H.C.CASSERLEY**

The High Girders – well, fairly high... 55238 heads the 4.55pm Oban-Ballachulish across Connel Ferry Bridge on 14 May 1960. In the far distance on the opposite bank of the loch is the slipway which was used by the ferry which had operated before the construction of the bridge. PHOTOGRAPH: W.A.C.SMITH

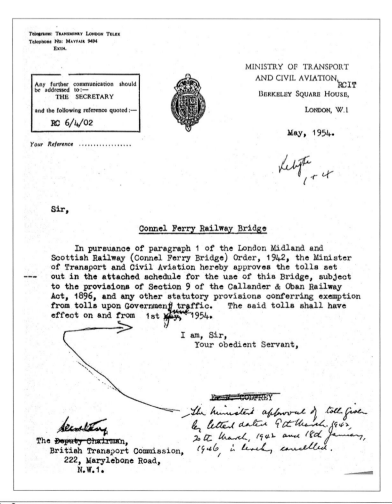

Telegrams: TRANSMINRY LONDON TELEX
Telephone No: MAYFAIR 9494
EXTN.

Any further communication should
be addressed to:—
THE SECRETARY

and the following reference quoted:—

RC 6/4/02

Your Reference ....

MINISTRY OF TRANSPORT
AND CIVIL AVIATION, RCIT
BERKELEY SQUARE HOUSE,
LONDON, W.1

May, 1954.

Sir,

Connel Ferry Railway Bridge

In pursuance of paragraph 1 of the London Midland and Scottish Railway (Connel Ferry Bridge) Order, 1942, the Minister of Transport and Civil Aviation hereby approves the tolls set out in the attached schedule for the use of this Bridge, subject to the provisions of Section 9 of the Callander & Oban Railway Act, 1896, and any other statutory provisions conferring exemption from tolls upon Government traffic. The said tolls shall have effect on and from 1st June, 1954.

I am, Sir,
Your obedient Servant,

GODFREY

The Deputy Chairman,
British Transport Commission,
222, Marylebone Road,
N.W.1.

The Minister's approval of tolls given by letters dated 9th March 1942, 20th March, 1942 and 18th January, 1946, is hereby cancelled.

NOTE OF MEETING ON 20th APRIL AT 203 BUCHANAN STREET, GLASGOW

Representations to the Scottish Area Board of the British Transport Commission by the Connel Ferry Bridge Tolls Committee supported by the Advisory Panel of the Highlands and Islands, The Scottish Tourist Board, Argyll County Council and others.

Present:

Scottish Area Board	Sir Ian Bolton, (Chairman)
	Sir Hugh Rose
	Lt. Col. D.H. Cameron of Lochiel
	Mr. Meldrum
	Mr. T.F. Cameron (Chief Regional Officer)
	Mr. H.M. Herbert (Secretary)
Connel Ferry Tolls Committee	Colonel Campbell-Preston (Chairman)
	Mr. A.F. Struthers (Messrs. J. & A. Gardner & Co. Ltd.).
	Major J.G. Struthers
	Mr. J. MacConnell Orr (Hon. Secretary)
Highlands Panel	Mr. John McNaughton
	Mr. T.M. Martin
Scottish Tourist Board	Mr. Ferris
National Union of General & Municipal Workers	Mr. Lyle

1. Colonel Campbell Preston introducing the deputation and expressing the general purposes, said that the Committee had been very disappointed that, following their representations earlier, only the very minor toll concessions of May 1954 had been made. They understood that the present Minister of Transport had indicated that nothing further could be done meantime from the Government side and that the matter was now one for the British Transport Commission to consider. He mentioned the various bodies which give strong support to the Committee, including the Highlands Panel, representatives of which were present.

No similar toll, so far as he knew, existed on any other trunk road in Great Britain. During the last twenty years there had been considerable development in the area; in the Alginate industry with a factory at Barcaldine; the Quarries at Bonawe; and in the development of farming, in respect of which Hill Farming Schemes in the area between Loch Creran and Loch Etive amounted to no less than £100,000. More cattle were being maintained, requiring the import of greater quantities of hay and other feeding materials. The present tolls on the Bridge, so far as heavy traffic was concerned, imposed a heavy burden on these industries and had a restrictive effect on development. In the case of Bonawe Quarries the toll charge represented approximately 25% of the cost of manufacture, which made the price of material transported across the Bridge prohibitive. Alginate Industries had considered extensions at their Barcaldine factory but because of the transport burden, decided that these extensions should be carried out at their Girvan factory. Two building firms operating on the north side of Connel Ferry, had closed down in recent years, primarily because of the transport costs. There was a possibility of developing clay deposits at Benderloch but development would be possible only if quick and cheap road transport were available. The concessions which had been made were of restricted value only, and did not ease in any way the burden on heavy industry, farming and tourism. He understood that the road bridge produced a revenue of about £13,000 a year which meant that the road bridge users were meeting a part of the deficit on the railway system of the whole area.

Mr. Struthers said that approximately £100,000 had been invested in Plant since the War for the new Brickworks development at Bonawe. Originally the Quarry material had been exported in small ships but since the opening of the Bridge to commercial traffic, markets on the south side had been tapped. The firm could not compete with firms elsewhere in disposing of their bricks and quarry products because of the additional burden of the tolls. His Company had been considering whether to revive a motor car ferry at Bonawe which had been operating up to the War, but, although prepared to incur an outlay of something like £5,000 on this Scheme, he would prefer that the brick and other products should go directly by road over the road bridge. He appealed for concessions for heavy industry as had been made for the smaller industries, whether through season ticket arrangements or otherwise.

Mr. Ferris speaking for the Scottish Tourist Board, said that it had been estimated that £44 million was spent on tourism in Scotland and the Board were anxious that tourist traffic should be facilitated in all parts of the country. The Connel Ferry road tolls were the only tolls of the kind in Scotland. The Board would be very glad to hear of any solution for the abolition of the tolls if some method could be found of meeting the loss to the British Transport Commission.

Mr. McNaughton speaking for the Highlands Panel, said that as early as 1947 the Panel had adopted the principle that there should be no tolls on the trunk roads. The Panel were not unaware of the difficulties of the Commission's position, who had, more or less by chance, inherited a connecting link between two trunk roads. The present tolls had a restrictive effect on industries in the area and the Panel would support anything which would help the industries; and if the Panel supported the plea for concessions it was clearly without prejudice to their view that tolls should be completely abolished. The Panel recognised that the British Transport Commission should not be asked to subsidise local industries by giving uneconomic toll concessions; it was primarily a road question and, ultimately, one for the Minister of Transport.

Many people had advocated that there should be a new independent bridge; but he thought it would be a matter for regret if expenditure from National Funds had to be incurred when there was already a bridge link between the two trunk roads. He was not aware what the Commission's reaction would be to a proposal to buy out the tolls, if such a proposal were made by the Minister of Transport. The Panel had been told that the buying out of the tolls could not be considered meantime but that did not mean to say such a proposal might not be deemed justified in the future.

The Panel were primarily interested in the prosperity of the area as a whole, as part of the Highlands; it was not their function to make a plea for particular industries but they did support the Connel Ferry Tolls Committee because the easing of the toll burden would benefit employment, and social conditions, in a large area.

A railway service was essential for the area, and B.T.C. had to work their undertaking efficiently; but if nothing was done to ease the present burden of the tolls there would certainly be pressure for something to be done to remove this anomaly. He recalled that the Report of the Committee on Ferries (1948) had suggested that the needs of the area would be met by abolishing the tolls on Connel Bridge, and that for that reason a ferry at Bonawe was not necessary.

The Panel would be glad to know whether the British Transport Commission would be prepared to agree in principle to the abolition of the tolls, whether by their being bought out or otherwise. The Panel had no knowledge of the Commission's attitude to any proposals which would involve their surrendering the tolls.

Mr. Lyle, National Union of General and Municipal Workers, supported the Committee. The toll charges were detrimental to increased productivity in the area and his Union give their full support to any measure which would increase employment.

In reply to Cameron of Lochiel, Mr. Struthers said that tolls cost his firm at least £1,500 a year. This was not transport business which was being lost to the railway because the bricks, etc. would have to be delivered by road in any case. There was ample opportunity for development of the brick industry; there were 50 empty houses available for more workers, but expansion was not possible unless the firm could compete on better terms.

Sir Ian Bolton told Mr. McNaughton that the Minister of Transport had never, so far as he knew, said anything to the Commission about buying out the tolls. What the attitude of his colleagues on the Board would be to such a proposal he did not know, but as the question had been put to them they would consider it. Mr. McNaughton said he assumed that the Board would consult the Commission before announcing any decision and Sir Ian Bolton undertook, at Mr. McNaughton's request, to let the Panel know the result of the Area Board's consideration. Mr. McNaughton said that the Panel's understanding was that, although the Minister may not have made any statement about his power, or willingness, to buy out the tolls, the fact that he had not denied having power to do so was significant.

Sir Ian Bolton said that he, personally, was very willing to consider the buying out of the tolls but he was in no position to commit his colleagues or the Commission.

Colonel Campbell-Preston summed up by saying that at their previous meeting with the then Minister of Transport (Mr. A. Lennox-Boyd) the Minister had himself suggested that the tolls might be bought out or leased from British Railways. Meantime the Bridge Committee while maintaining the principle of total abolition, would welcome any worthwhile concession. The matter was urgent and he hoped the Area Board would go to the utmost limit to meet the Committee's representations.

Sir Ian Bolton promised that the Area Board would consider the representations that had been made and would let their decision be known in due course.

British Transport Commission meeting, 20 April 1955.

The 3.45pm from Ballachulish approaches the north end of the bridge on 19 April 1952. Almost out of view at the front is Caley 0-4-4T 55196. PHOTOGRAPH: H.C.CASSERLEY

101 uses for a dead shed
Photographs from the Transport Treasury

And finally...

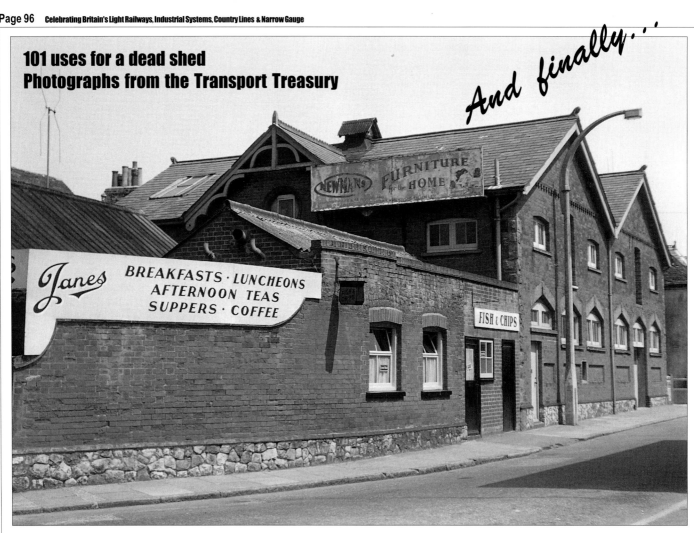

We've seen disused engine sheds which have put to all manner of commercial uses, but how about one which became, at least in part, a restaurant and a chippy? Yes – this is the South Eastern Railway's old tramcar depot at Hythe in Kent. The premises date back to 1891 when the SER opened the horse-worked tramway linking the centre of Hythe, the Imperial Hotel on the sea front on the outskirts of Hythe, Sandgate station and the town of Sandgate. The tramway closed in 1914 after its horses had been requisitioned by the War Office, but it reopened with ex-Army mules in 1919. The resuscitation was, however, brief, as the tramway closed again in 1921, this time for good. The old tramcar shed and stables at Hythe were put to good use, as evidenced in these pictures which we reckon were taken in the early 1960s. As can be seen in the lower picture, the tramway building's origins are still evident – the legend 'S.E.R. Folkestone Hythe & Sandgate Tramways' is clearly discernible on the main building.